Farm Journal's Best-Ever Recipes

Recipes in this book were selected by homemakers from the following Farm Journal cookbooks:

Farm Journal's Country Cookbook

Farm Journal's Timesaving Country Cookbook

Freezing & Canning Cookbook

Farm Journal's Complete Pie Cookbook

Let's Start To Cook

Cooking For Company

Homemade Bread

America's Best Vegetable Recipes

Homemade Candy

Busy Woman's Cookbook
Timesaving Cookbook—Revised

Homemade Cookies

Farm Journal's Country Cookbook
Revised Enlarged Edition

Homemade Ice Cream And Cake

Family Favorites From Country Kitchens

Informal Entertaining Country Style
Cooking For Company—Revised

Freezing & Canning Cookbook
Revised Edition

Everyday Cooking With Herbs

The Thrifty Cook

Country Fair Cookbook

Great Home Cooking In America

Farm Journal's Best-Ever Recipes

Edited by ELISE W. MANNING
FARM JOURNAL FOOD EDITOR

COUNTRYSIDE PRESS
A division of Farm Journal, Inc.
Philadelphia, Pennsylvania

Distributed to the trade by
DOUBLEDAY & COMPANY, INC., Garden City, New York

Book Design, Drawings: Maureen Sweeney

ISBN: 0-385-12966-1
Library of Congress Catalog Card Number 76-55041

Farm Journal's Best-Ever Recipes

COLOR ILLUSTRATIONS

CONTENTS

Farm Journal's Best-Ever Recipes

Every good cook has at least a few recipes that never fail her, and never fail to win praise from family or guests. Such recipes become prized possessions and, chances are, she knows every one of them by heart.

Through the years so many women have told us that their most-relied-on recipe came from a FARM JOURNAL cookbook that we decided to "call the roll" and find out what kinds of recipes enjoy this exalted status. We wrote to 250,000 of our cookbook users, asking them to tell us their top favorite recipe from any of our cookbooks, and why. Response was enthusiastic and ranged the entire menu—from main dishes to desserts—with recipes in every category and from every one of the books. What surprised us was the interesting assortment of pickle and vegetable recipes since these seldom seem to be regarded as a cook's specialty.

We counted the votes and present to you here the recipes with which a quarter of a million American women have their greatest success. That's a pretty good reason for you to try them and a guarantee that your rewards will be smiles around the table, certain flattery from family and guests, and requests for "let's have that again."

Most of these recipes, as is the case in all our cookbooks, originated in farm kitchens. Country women have always been known for their good home cooking, for their ability to improvise—to take a few ingredients and with imagination and ingenuity come up with an outstanding dish to feed a hungry family.

Actually this goes back to pioneer days, when farm women lived from their land. They made use of their own hand-churned butter, of milk and cream, eggs, chickens, beef, pork and bounty from their fields and orchards. They had to be thrifty and put food by in the summer and fall to take them through the long cold winters. There were no grocery stores around the corner—they made do with what was on hand.

A primary concern of farm women was to feed the family well, and when husbands and children praised their cooking, they glowed with pride. Women carefully copied down each other's recipes to please their families, but some special recipes for which they had acquired an envious reputation remained secret treasures. Hospitality to farm women meant coffee or tea and always something to eat—even invitations to "stay for dinner" at the last minute. They cooked in quantity for crews of hungry harvesters.

Today's farm women are no different from their pioneer great-grandmothers in how they feel about cooking. They take the same pride in serving delicious, home-cooked food, in sharing with friends and neighbors; they are proud of their reputations for making the best baked beans for the church supper or the finest doughnuts for the bake sale.

Good farm cooks have been sharing their recipes with FARM JOURNAL for almost a century. We have tested and shared them in turn with millions of homemakers—both country and urban—throughout the USA by publishing cookbooks which reflect the superior cooking in farm kitchens.

Our cookbook users tell us time and time again of certain favorite recipes they acquired from FARM JOURNAL cookbooks. They'll say that the Brown-Butter Butterscotch Pie, page 119 in *Farm Journal's Complete Pie Cookbook,* is the smoothest satiny-textured pie they have ever made; that the doughnuts from *Country Fair Cookbook,* page 55, won 30 blue ribbons at fairs in the last six years; that Cucumber-Sour Cream Salad, page 207 in *America's Best Vegetables Recipes,* is a must at family reunions; that the *Freezing and Canning Cookbook* is their bible during summer and fall.

In one community the supper held each autumn has been made famous by the Chicken-Rice Bake recipe on page 60 in *Cooking for Company.* The recipe for Cabbage-Onion Salad on page 117 in the same book is used over and over. As one farm homemaker wrote us, "This recipe stays at home, goes camping every year and travels to a great many community suppers. And my in-laws (who are hard to please) always request this salad when they come to visit."

FARM JOURNAL reaches its Centennial in the spring of 1977; the magazine was founded in 1877—100 years ago. What better way to celebrate with our millions of cookbook fans than to create and share one special book filled with the most cherished, most-used recipes women have selected from all our cookbooks. Who could better choose the best desserts, cookies, meats, breads and other favorites than our cookbook users themselves? The pie or pickle that husbands praised was a sure winner. So were breads—their fresh-baked fragrance brings the family hurrying to the kitchen for thick slices still warm from the oven. And if kids actually ask for seconds on vegetables, we were told which recipe was that successful.

Farm women registered their delight in finding a recipe that proves popular with everyone—and also promotes their farm products. They gladly copy off such recipes to give to their city friends—often accompanied by a sample.

Other reasons for naming favorites will sound familiar to most women who cook every day: "The recipe uses ingredients I almost always have on hand . . . It's quick and easy—but so good . . . It never, never fails me . . ." And many women thanked us for recipes that have earned them the reputation of outstanding cook in their community. They have taught their children to be outstanding cooks, too, with recipes from FARM JOURNAL cookbooks as their guide.

The cookbook owners we questioned averaged six of our cookbooks each. Many others had up to nine and a fairly large number had them all. Yet, they still say they will be eagerly awaiting the publication of *Farm Journal's Best-Ever Recipes* all contained in one book to see what other families rate tops.

With each recipe submitted as the top favorite were comments from our cookbook users telling us exactly why they chose the particular recipe. We have selected some of these personal comments from homemakers to introduce each recipe to you. In this way you'll know what it is about the recipe that creates the enthusiasm for it. Sometimes a homemaker suggested useful adaptations she has made.

Often a woman told us of the pride she takes in serving her family great meals and watching their faces light up when she brings in one of their favorites. The Food Editors and Test Kitchen Staff of FARM JOURNAL take great pride in our cookbooks, too, and we hope that your face will light up as you browse through this book and share with great farm cooks all over the country the pleasure of preparing and serving these Best-Ever recipes.

MEATS
&
MAIN DISHES

MEATS & MAIN DISHES

SWISS STEAK
BEEF STROGANOFF
CALIFORNIA POT ROAST
COMPANY CORNED BEEF
MEATBALL STEW
SAVORY BEEF STEW
AFTER-CHURCH STEW
FOUR-HOUR BEEF STEW
MEATBALL CHOWDER
LASAGNE ROLL-UPS
BROWN STEW
MEAT LOAF
AMERICAN-STYLE ENCHILADAS
PORCUPINE MEATBALLS
BEEF-MACARONI SKILLET
PORK/SAUERKRAUT PINWHEEL
SAVORY SAUSAGE RICE
SWEET-SOUR PORK
SCALLOPED POTATOES
   WITH PORK CHOPS
CRUSTY FRIED CHICKEN
CHICKEN WITH DRESSING
CHICKEN-RICE BAKE
PAPRIKA CHICKEN
SUMMER CHICKEN WITH PEAS
CHICKEN WITH DUMPLINGS
MAINE CHICKEN PIE
CRISP OVEN-FRIED CHICKEN
SALMON LOAF WITH SHRIMP SAUCE

Meats And Main Dishes

Meat recipes come first in this FARM JOURNAL Best-Ever collection because more women nominated a meat or main dish recipe as their first-place favorite than any other single food category—even bread (which ran a close second).

Comments from farm women, of course, underline their dual interest as consumers and producers. "We're always searching for good recipes to use and to promote our farm products."

But every busy homemaker and mother—often a woman with an outside job, too—can appreciate the merits of "quick and easy main dishes to make ahead and freeze" and recipes "that can simmer or bake to perfection while I'm busy helping my husband or while we are at church." They are always on the lookout for recipes that are easy, economical and can be stretched to feed unexpected guests.

Discovering a good main dish—one the family applauds—is more than a triumph in taste. It also means you've made your major decision on the day's menu. Many of the notes in this chapter suggest the good go-withs that hostesses serve with the meat platter for their favorite company dinners—and for family meals, too.

Women had high praise for the recipes they call one-dish dinners: all the stews and skillets and casseroles that combine meat, potatoes and vegetables with just the right seasonings. Read their comments to see which ones they fix for company buffets, for the gourmet cooking club or the first night camping.

New and different ways to use ground beef rated high with all busy wives who like to feed their families well but economically. Chicken, too, is reasonable the year round and women found many chicken recipes in FARM JOURNAL cookbooks to praise. Old-fashioned Chicken with Dumplings and Chicken with Dressing rated high with homemakers. A top favorite for company meals, Summer Chicken with Peas, uses ingredients that are part of the bounty of our land, several farm women wrote us.

Browse through these pages and see what experienced cooks recommend for nourishing meals that prompt the reward: "Boy, this is good, Mom."

This superb Swiss Steak cooks to perfection while we are at church. When I get home, I toss a salad and cook a vegetable and dinner is ready to serve a hungry family. (Alabama) □We raise our own beef—this is our most favorite recipe to serve to city friends when they come to our farm. Best beef dish they have ever had, they all agree. (Wisconsin) □I have made this with moose meat with equally good results. Even those who don't care for game like it fixed this way. (Ohio) □A great dish to freeze and have on hand for the busy season. The field crew rate this as one of their top favorites. (Kansas)

SWISS STEAK

2 lbs. round steak, cut 1-inch thick
¼ c. flour
2 tsp. salt
¼ tsp. pepper
⅓ c. cooking oil
4 medium onions, sliced
½ c. chopped celery
1 clove garlic, minced
¾ c. chili sauce
¾ c. water
1 medium green pepper, seeded and
   sliced in rings

Dredge round steak with combined flour, salt and pepper. Brown in hot oil in 12-inch skillet, removing meat as it browns. Add onion. Saute until lightly browned.

Return meat to skillet. Add celery, garlic, chili sauce, water and green pepper. Bring to a boil; reduce heat. Cover and simmer 1 hour or until meat is tender. Makes 6 servings.

We raise our own beef—Beef Stroganoff is our pet recipe to serve to company, inexpensive but gourmet. (North Dakota) □Farm Journal's recipe for stroganoff is the first one I reach for when I'm planning a company dinner. I know it will always be a success. (Pennsylvania) □I make this with round steak as well as sirloin. Men in my family love this with wild rice or mashed potatoes. (California)

BEEF STROGANOFF

1½ lbs. boneless sirloin steak, cut in
   1x¼-inch strips
3½ tblsp. flour
¼ c. butter or regular margarine
1 c. chopped onion
1 (10½ oz.) can condensed
   beef bouillon
1 tblsp. Worcestershire sauce
1 tsp. salt
½ tsp. dry mustard
2 tblsp. tomato paste
1 c. dairy sour cream
1 (4 oz.) can chopped mushrooms,
   drained

Dredge sirloin steak with flour; reserve remaining flour. Brown quickly in melted butter in 12-inch skillet. Add onion and cook 3 to 4 minutes.

Remove meat and onion from skillet. Blend reserved flour into pan drippings in skillet. Cook over medium heat 1 minute, stirring constantly. Stir in beef bouillon and Worcestershire sauce. Cook, stirring constantly, until thickened. Stir in salt, mustard and tomato paste. Blend in sour cream. Add meat and mushrooms. Cool quickly.

Pour into freezer containers. Seal and freeze. Recommended storage: 3 to 6 months.

To Serve: Partially thaw in refrigerator. Heat in top of double boiler until hot. Delicious served over rice or noodles. Makes 5 cups or 6 servings.

I adapted this California Pot Roast recipe for my pressure cooker. A quick-to-fix meal for last-minute guests that always draws compliments and recipe requests. (Ohio) ☐This roast is the highlight of any company buffet menu. It's fantastic when made with venison. (Montana) ☐Our freezer is stocked with beef. We think this recipe is a great treat and so do our guests. It's tender, tasty and different. (California)

CALIFORNIA POT ROAST

4 to 5 lb. chuck or rump pot roast
3 tblsp. cooking oil
2 tsp. salt
¼ tsp. pepper
½ c. water
1 (8 oz.) can tomato sauce
3 medium onions, thinly sliced
2 cloves garlic, minced
2 tblsp. brown sugar, firmly packed
½ tsp. dry mustard
¼ c. lemon juice
¼ c. vinegar
¼ c. ketchup
1 tblsp. Worcestershire sauce
6 tblsp. flour
½ c. water

Brown roast on all sides in hot oil in Dutch oven. Add salt, pepper, ½ c. water, tomato sauce, onion and garlic. Bring to a boil; reduce heat. Cover and simmer 1½ hours.

Combine brown sugar, mustard, lemon juice, vinegar, ketchup and Worcestershire sauce; pour over meat. Cover; simmer 1½ hours or until tender.

Remove meat to warm platter. Skim off most of the fat; measure broth. Add enough water to broth to make 3 c. Return liquid to Dutch oven. Mix flour with ½ c. water in small bowl to make a smooth paste. Stir into broth. Cook, stirring constantly, until mixture comes to a boil. Boil 1 minute. Slice roast and serve with gravy. Makes 8 to 10 servings.

Company Corned Beef is such a different recipe for fixing corned beef. It's tasty and economical—great sliced the next day for sandwiches. My favorite recipe when we are hungry for corned beef. (California)   □This recipe is a nice change from the traditional corned beef. I serve German potato salad with it for Fourth of July picnics. (Indiana)   □This is one of those tantalizing dishes that smell so good while cooking. The family always queries when I'm fixing this beef—how soon before dinner? (Oregon)   □I always double this recipe and if there is any left over, the family fights over who will be the lucky one to eat it. (Kansas)

COMPANY CORNED BEEF

4 to 5 lbs. corned beef
2 bay leaves
5 peppercorns
2 sprigs fresh parsley
1 stalk celery, cut in chunks
1 small onion, sliced
Whole cloves
2 tblsp. butter or regular margarine
1 tblsp. prepared mustard
⅓ c. brown sugar, firmly packed
⅓ c. ketchup
3 tblsp. vinegar
3 tblsp. water

Wash corned beef thoroughly to remove brine. Place in large kettle; cover with cold water. Add bay leaves, peppercorns, parsley, celery and onion. Bring to a boil; reduce heat. Cover and simmer 3½ hours or until meat is tender.

Remove beef to shallow baking dish. Insert whole cloves in it.

Melt butter in saucepan; add remaining ingredients and mix thoroughly. Cook over medium heat 5 minutes, stirring occasionally. Pour sauce over corned beef.

Bake in 350° oven 30 minutes, basting with the sauce several times. Serve hot or cold. Makes 8 to 10 servings.

Meatball Stew is an easy, economical, make-ahead meal in one dish. (Kansas)   □This stew is so versatile. Can be made in a hurry or can simmer in a slow cooker. (Utah)   □I serve this when my husband has businessmen in for dinner. It can be stretched to serve several unexpected guests, too. Most important, the men like it; even the non-stew-lovers come back for seconds! (Montana)

MEATBALL STEW

1½ lbs. ground beef
1½ tsp. salt
⅛ tsp. pepper
1 egg
1 tblsp. minced onion
½ c. soft bread crumbs
1 tblsp. cooking oil
3 tblsp. flour
1 (1 lb.) can tomatoes, cut up
1 c. water
½ tsp. salt
2 tsp. sugar
1 tsp. basil leaves
3 medium potatoes, pared and diced
4 small carrots, pared and diced
1 medium onion, coarsely chopped
1 stalk celery, sliced

Combine ground beef, 1½ tsp. salt, pepper, egg, onion and bread crumbs in bowl; mix lightly but well. Form mixture into 1-inch meatballs. Brown meatballs, on all sides, in hot oil in 10-inch skillet. Remove meatballs as they brown; place in 2-qt. casserole. Pour off fat, reserving 3 tblsp. Blend flour into reserved fat in skillet. Stir in tomatoes, water, ½ tsp. salt, sugar and basil; stir well. Add potatoes, carrots, onion and celery. Bring to a boil; reduce heat and simmer 10 minutes, adding more water if necessary. Pour over meatballs in casserole. Cover.

Bake in 350° oven 1 hour or until vegetables are tender. Makes 6 servings.

Salmon Loaf with Shrimp Sauce—recipe, page 50

Meatball Stew—recipe, page 20

Savory Beef Stew—recipe, page 23

Just can't beat Savory Beef Stew for a company meal. (Iowa) □When I tell my guests we're having stew for dinner, they think it's going to be the same nondescript stew they have at home. Are they ever surprised! They tell me that it doesn't even taste like stew. (Illinois) □I served this to our Gourmet Cooking Club and everyone wanted the recipe. (Ohio) □Wonderful to take to a potluck and equally good to serve at home. It's the only stew my family will eat. (New York)

SAVORY BEEF STEW

2 lbs. stewing beef, cut in 1-inch
  cubes
¼ c. cooking oil
1½ c. chopped onion
1 (1 lb.) can tomatoes, cut up
3 tblsp. quick-cooking tapioca
1 (10½ oz.) can condensed beef
  broth
1 clove garlic, minced
1 tblsp. parsley flakes
2½ tsp. salt
¼ tsp. pepper
1 bay leaf
6 medium carrots, pared and cut
  in strips
3 medium potatoes, pared and
  quartered
½ c. sliced celery

Brown beef cubes on all sides in hot oil in large skillet. Add onion, tomatoes, tapioca, beef broth, garlic, parsley, salt, pepper and bay leaf. Bring mixture to a boil. Turn into 3-qt. casserole. Cover.

Bake in 350° oven for 1 hour 30 minutes or until meat is tender.

Add carrots, potatoes and celery. Continue baking, covered, for 1 hour or until vegetables are tender. Makes 6 to 8 servings.

After-Church Stew—a hearty delicious dish to serve to a hungry crowd after the football game. (Minnesota) □As a busy dairy farmer's wife, I find little time to fix fancy dishes but like to serve something special. My family thinks this is extra-special. (New York) □After-Church Stew—I just pop this in the oven and forget it. (Kansas) □My husband and four sons can finish a double batch of this stew at one sitting. In fact, it's their favorite after-church dinner. (Michigan) □Whenever I am asked to take a dish to a bridal shower, I always choose After-Church Stew and give the recipe to the bride-to-be. (Ohio)

AFTER-CHURCH STEW

1½ lbs. lean beef, cut in 1½-inch
   cubes (chuck, round or top sirloin)
2 tsp. salt
½ tsp. basil leaves
¼ tsp. pepper
2 stalks celery, cut in diagonal slices
4 medium carrots, pared and
   quartered
2 medium onions, cut in ½-inch
   slices
1 (10¾ oz.) can condensed tomato
   soup
½ soup can water
3 medium potatoes, pared and cubed

Place beef (no need to brown it) in 3-qt. casserole. Sprinkle with salt, basil and pepper. Top with celery, carrots and onions.

Combine soup and water. Pour over meat and vegetables, coating all pieces. Cover tightly. Bake in slow 300° oven 3 hours.

Add potatoes and bake 45 minutes longer. Makes 5 servings.

Four-Hour Beef Stew is a no-watch nutritious dinner the whole family likes. (Iowa) □Requires little attention and is delicious. (Nebraska) □A timesaver recipe for me because it is not necessary to brown the meat—this saves a lot of time and clean-up. It's a dish I'm proud to serve to my family, hired men and company. (Kansas) □This stew is our traditional first-day-camping meal. I freeze it ahead and while we are having our swim, the stew is simmering, ready to eat when we return to the camp site. (Minnesota)

FOUR-HOUR BEEF STEW

1½ lbs. lean stewing beef, cut in
   1-inch cubes
3 medium potatoes, pared and
   quartered
6 medium carrots, pared and cut in
   1-inch pieces
2 medium onions, quartered
1 c. sliced celery
2 tsp. seasoned salt
⅛ tsp. pepper
1 (15 oz.) can tomato sauce
1 c. water
¼ c. flour
½ c. water

Combine beef, potatoes, carrots, onions and celery in Dutch oven. Sprinkle with seasoned salt and pepper. Pour on tomato sauce and 1 c. water; stir to mix. Cover.

Bake in 275° oven 4 hours. Remove from oven; place on range top.

Combine flour and ½ c. water in small bowl; blend until smooth. Add to stew; cook until liquid thickens, stirring often. Makes 6 servings.

Meatball Chowder tastes even better when it's reheated. And that's important to me as I often serve two suppers, one at 5 o'clock for the kids, another three hours later for my weary and hungry husband and field crew. (New Hampshire) □We always take a double recipe of Meatball Chowder when we go hunting. And during the winter months, I make this at least once a week for the family—they never tire of Mom's Chowder. (Idaho) □Makes enough to feed a crowd. I don't make the meat into balls but just brown it and add the remaining ingredients—that's the way my family likes it. (Utah)

MEATBALL CHOWDER

2 lbs. ground lean beef
2 tsp. seasoned salt
⅛ tsp. pepper
2 eggs, slightly beaten
¼ c. finely chopped fresh parsley
⅓ c. fine cracker crumbs
2 tblsp. milk
3 tblsp. flour
1 tblsp. cooking oil
4 to 6 onions, cut in eighths
6 c. water
6 c. tomato juice
6 beef bouillon cubes
3 c. sliced pared carrots (about 6)
3 to 4 c. sliced celery
2 to 3 c. diced pared potatoes
¼ c. regular rice
1 tblsp. sugar
2 tsp. salt
2 bay leaves
1 tsp. marjoram leaves
1 (12 oz.) can Mexicorn

Combine ground beef, seasoned salt, pepper, eggs, parsley, cracker crumbs and milk. Mix thoroughly. Form into 1-inch meatballs. Dip in flour.

Brown meatballs in hot oil in 8-qt. kettle. Add remaining ingredients. Cover and simmer 30 minutes or until vegetables are tender. Makes 6 quarts.

Lasagne Roll-Ups—recipe, page 28

Lasagne Roll-Ups are a big favorite with our teen-agers. Our 17-year-old son likes them so well I have learned to triple the recipe. He always gives me a compliment and a hug when I fix it for him. (Washington) □A good-sized tasty casserole that's a treat for our teen-agers—adults like it, too. (Minnesota) □This dish is speedy to make, but looks as if you spent hours fixing it—impressive for company. (Ohio) □When I first read the recipe, I hesitated to make it, thought it would be complicated—but it was so easy to do. The sauce has a unique flavor, much tastier than most sauces for lasagne. (Wyoming)

LASAGNE ROLL-UPS

Meat Sauce (recipe follows)
Ricotta Filling (recipe follows)
1 (1 lb.) pkg. lasagne noodles,
   cooked and drained
⅔ c. hot water

Prepare Meat Sauce and Ricotta Filling.

Rinse drained noodles in cold water. Drain well. Blot with paper towels. Spread ¼ c. Ricotta Filling on each noodle. Fold over 1-inch and continue to fold, making a slightly flat roll. Repeat with remaining noodles.

Place 1 c. Meat Sauce in each of two 11x7x1½-inch baking dishes. Place 8 roll-ups, seam side down, in each. Add half of hot water to each dish. Pour over enough Meat Sauce to almost cover roll-ups; reserve remaining sauce.

Bake in 350° oven 35 minutes or until hot and bubbly. Serve roll-ups with remaining sauce. Makes 16 roll-ups or 8 servings.

MEAT SAUCE

1½ lbs. ground beef
⅓ c. cooking oil
⅓ c. finely chopped onion
2 cloves garlic, minced
2 tsp. salt
¼ tsp. pepper
2 whole cloves
½ bay leaf
2 (1 lb. 1 oz.) cans plum tomatoes
2 (6 oz.) cans tomato paste
1¼ c. water
1 tsp. oregano leaves
2 tsp. sugar

Brown ground beef in hot oil in Dutch oven. When meat begins to turn color, add onion, garlic, salt, pepper, cloves and bay leaf. Saute until meat is well-browned.

Press tomatoes through a sieve or whirl in blender until smooth. Add tomatoes, tomato paste, water, oregano and sugar to Dutch oven. Simmer, covered loosely, 1 hour; stirring occasionally.

RICOTTA FILLING

2 lbs. ricotta cheese
½ tsp. salt
⅛ tsp. pepper
½ tsp. ground nutmeg
¼ lb. mozzarella cheese, shredded
4 tblsp. grated Parmesan cheese
1 tblsp. chopped fresh parsley

Whip ricotta cheese in bowl until smooth. Add salt, pepper, nutmeg, cheeses and parsley; mix well.

Brown Stew for supper transforms a cold winter night into a blessing. (Iowa) □I call this my man-pleaser stew. My husband likes it even better the second time around. (Colorado) □Browning the meat gives this stew extra-good flavor. I have served it many times to company and they love it. Piping hot garlic bread and homemade apple pie round out the meal. (Oregon) □We raise beef cattle and this is my husband's favorite way to cook some of his grain-fed beef for city friends. (North Carolina) □After a long day of hunting, this stew really makes a hit with everyone. (Idaho)

BROWN STEW

2 lbs. beef chuck, cut in 1½-inch
   cubes
3 tblsp. cooking oil
1 clove garlic, cut in half
2 tsp. salt
¼ tsp. pepper
1 tsp. Worcestershire sauce
1 tsp. lemon juice
1 small bay leaf
2 c. water
3 potatoes, pared and halved
4 carrots, pared and cut in thirds
1 c. cubed celery (1-inch pieces)
2 c. water
1 c. cooked lima beans
1 c. cooked peas
¼ c. flour
½ c. water

Brown beef cubes on all sides in hot oil in 4-qt. Dutch oven. Add garlic; saute 1 minute. Add salt, pepper, Worcestershire sauce, lemon juice, bay leaf and 2 c. water. Bring to a boil; reduce heat. Cover and simmer 2 hours, stirring occasionally.

Remove bay leaf. Add potatoes, carrots, celery and 2 c. water. Continue cooking 30 minutes or until vegetables are tender. Add lima beans and peas. Combine flour and ½ c. water; blend well. Stir into stew. Cook 1 minute to thicken. Makes 8 servings.

My nine-year-old daughter always tells me that this Meat Loaf is the very best she has ever eaten—and she's a fussy eater. (Missouri) □An economical, easy and very good loaf. I sometimes add cheese for variation. (Nebraska) □My husband doesn't compliment my cooking very often but he always says "Boy, this is good meat loaf." That makes my day. (Wisconsin) □A flavorful, moist loaf. I have added green pepper and omitted the chili powder. (Illinois) □A loaf that can be dressed up for company. It's also great for sandwiches or for supper on Saturday nights with a pot of bubbling hot baked beans. (Indiana)

MEAT LOAF

2 lbs. ground beef
1 medium onion, sliced
2 eggs
1½ tsp. dry mustard
1 tsp. chili powder
1½ c. stewed tomatoes
2 slices bread, broken into pieces
2 tsp. salt
¼ tsp. pepper
4 strips bacon

Combine ground beef, onion, eggs, dry mustard, chili powder, tomatoes, bread, salt and pepper in large bowl. Mix lightly, but well. Pack mixture into 9x5x3-inch loaf pan. Place bacon strips across top.

Bake in 350° oven 1 hour and 30 minutes or until well-browned. Makes 8 to 10 servings.

My family never knew spinach could taste so good until I served American-Style Enchiladas. This is even better when it's served the second time. (Iowa) □This dish looks so elegant I can't believe I made it. (California) □We have used this recipe to promote farm commodities in a food demonstration. I have served this dish for harvest and haying meals and at covered dish suppers. It has become an old faithful in my meal planning—lots of nourishment at low cost. (Illinois) □I have served this as the main dish for teen-age parties—never saw anything disappear so fast. (Ohio)

AMERICAN-STYLE ENCHILADAS

Thin Pancakes (recipe follows)
1 lb. ground beef
1 lb. bulk pork sausage
1 c. chopped onion
½ c. chopped green pepper
2 cloves garlic, minced
1⅔ tblsp. chili powder
1 tsp. salt
1 (10 oz.) pkg. frozen spinach,
　　cooked, drained and chopped
1 (29 oz.) jar or 2 (15 oz.) cans
　　meatless spaghetti sauce
1 (8 oz.) can tomato sauce
1 c. water
1 tblsp. chili powder
2 c. shredded Cheddar cheese

Prepare Thin Pancakes.

Brown ground beef and pork sausage in large skillet. Pour off all but 1 tblsp. fat. Add onion, green pepper, garlic, 1⅔ tblsp. chili powder and salt. Simmer for 10 minutes. Add spinach; mix well. Let cool.

Combine spaghetti sauce, tomato sauce, water and 1 tblsp. chili powder; set aside.

Spoon scant ¼ c. meat mixture across center of each pancake. Fold sides over about ½-inch. Starting at end closest to you, roll up each pancake. Place in two 13x9x2-inch baking dishes. Pour half of the sauce over the rolled pancakes in each baking dish. Top each with half of shredded cheese.

Bake in 325° oven 30 minutes or until hot and bubbly. Makes 15 servings.

Note: Prepared Enchiladas can be frozen. To re-heat: Bake in 375° oven 45 minutes or until hot.

THIN PANCAKES

6 eggs, well beaten
3 c. milk
2 c. sifted flour
¾ tsp. salt

Combine eggs and milk in bowl. Add flour and salt; beat until smooth. Pour about ¼ c. batter into hot greased 6 to 7-inch skillet, tilting skillet so batter covers surface. Batter can also be spread into 6-inch rounds on greased griddle. Turn pancakes when the surface looks dry. Pancakes can be stacked while remaining pancakes are baked. Makes 30.

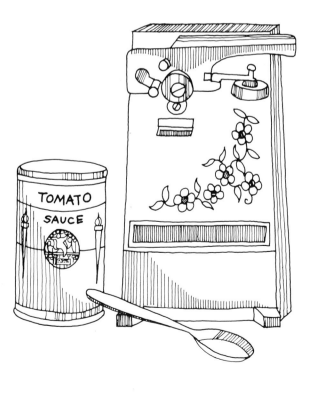

Porcupine Meatballs is my favorite dish to serve hungry men. I've made it many times and it's always a success with both children and adults. (Michigan)   □I like this recipe because I can make the meatballs ahead and freeze. Then I simply remove from the freezer, add the remaining ingredients and bake. My husband raves about this dish. (Virginia)   □I double this for a buffet company meal or our annual camping trip. So easy to make as there's no need to brown the meatballs in a skillet—saves time and bother. (Kansas)   □Since we raise our own beef, I'm always looking for ground beef recipes that are different and take little time to prepare—this recipe fills the bill. (Pennsylvania)

PORCUPINE MEATBALLS

1½ lbs. ground beef
½ c. regular rice
⅔ c. milk
1 tblsp. instant minced onion or
    1 medium onion, chopped
1½ tsp. salt
¼ tsp. pepper
1 (10½ oz.) can condensed tomato
    soup
¾ c. water

Combine ground beef, rice, milk, minced onion, salt and pepper in bowl. Mix lightly, but well. Drop rounded tablespoonfuls of mixture into 13x9x2-inch baking pan.

Combine tomato soup and water in bowl; mix well. Pour over meatballs. Cover baking pan tightly with aluminum foil.

Bake in 350° oven 1 hour or until hot and bubbly. Makes 6 to 8 servings.

Beef-Macaroni Skillet is a lifesaver when I've forgotten to take meat from the freezer for dinner. It can be put together quickly and is so tasty. (Wisconsin) □A delicious dish that I can fix in a hurry and know my family will be happy with what they are having for supper. (Utah) □A real timesaver recipe. I like it because you don't have to bother to cook the macaroni separately. (Arkansas) □A meal that I can make in less than 30 minutes. These are the type of easy skillet dinners a busy farm woman appreciates. (Iowa) □A delicious, hearty dish that holds well when the men don't come in from the fields in time for dinner. (Indiana)

BEEF-MACARONI SKILLET

1 lb. ground beef
1 medium onion, chopped
3 c. tomato juice
1 tblsp. Worcestershire sauce
1 tblsp. vinegar
1 tsp. salt
⅛ tsp. pepper
1 tsp. dry mustard
1 c. uncooked elbow macaroni

Brown beef and onion in 12-inch skillet. Add tomato juice, Worcestershire sauce, vinegar, salt, pepper, mustard and macaroni. Bring to boil; reduce heat. Cover and simmer 20 minutes or until macaroni is tender. Stir occasionally during cooking. Makes 6 servings.

A wonderful make-ahead recipe for company. Pork/Sauerkraut Pinwheel is simple to make and so attractive. We serve it with whipped potatoes, green beans and fried apple rings. (Indiana)   □We're hog farmers and our friends expect us to serve pork in unusual and tasty ways. They're never disappointed when I present this dish—you should hear the appreciative comments as the platter is passed. (Ohio)   □We make our own sauerkraut and this dish is a perfect way to show it off—also no last-minute carving for my husband to worry about. (Iowa)

PORK/SAUERKRAUT PINWHEEL

2 lbs. ground lean pork
¾ c. dry bread crumbs
2 eggs, slightly beaten
⅓ c. milk
1½ tsp. salt
¼ tsp. pepper
1 tsp. thyme leaves
1 tblsp. Worcestershire sauce
1 (1 lb.) can sauerkraut, drained
¼ c. chopped onion
3 tblsp. chopped pimientos
1 tblsp. sugar
5 strips bacon

Combine ground pork, bread crumbs, eggs, milk, salt, pepper, thyme and Worcestershire sauce; mix lightly, but well. Pat pork mixture on waxed paper into 12x9-inch rectangle. Combine sauerkraut, onion, pimientos and sugar in bowl; mix well. Spread evenly over meat. Roll up from narrow end, using waxed paper to aid in rolling. Place loaf in greased 11x7x1½-inch baking dish. Lay bacon diagonally over top.

Bake in 375° oven 1 hour 10 minutes or until done. Makes 8 servings.

Savory Sausage Rice is tops and it uses a product from our farm—homemade pork sausage. I serve it for supper with fruit salad and muffins. (Iowa)   □This sausage dish travels with us on all our camping trips—I always plan enough for third helpings. (Missouri)   □We make our own pork sausage, but my kids aren't fond of sausage. They clean their plates, though, when I serve this savory dish—tastes different and good, they tell me. (Minnesota)   □We eat a lot of sausage and this recipe is a pleasant change from the usual patties and links. (Ohio) □Good old-fashioned flavor in an up-to-date dish. Makes a hit at our church suppers—I usually spend an hour writing down recipe requests! (Delaware)

SAVORY SAUSAGE RICE

2 lbs. bulk pork sausage
2½ c. coarsely chopped celery
1 c. finely chopped green pepper
¾ c. chopped onion
2 (2⅛ oz.) pkgs. chicken noodle
  soup mix
4½ c. boiling water
1 c. regular rice
1 c. blanched slivered almonds
¼ c. melted butter or margarine

Lightly brown sausage in Dutch oven; pour off excess fat. Add celery, green pepper and onion; saute until tender.

Combine soup mix and boiling water in 3-qt. saucepan. Stir in rice. Cover and simmer 15 minutes or until rice is tender. Add rice mixture to sausage; stir well. Pour into greased 13x9x2-inch baking dish. Sprinkle with almonds; drizzle with butter.

Bake in 375° oven 20 minutes or until hot. Makes 10 servings.

Sweet-Sour Pork has a perfect blending of seasonings and textures. It's so easy to fix and so versatile. This shows up often at our community dinners—it has really made the rounds in our town. (New York)   □There's a fine Chinese restaurant in our area that's noted for sweet-sour pork—but this recipe is even better than theirs. (California)   □I receive so many compliments when I serve this dish—it's a great way to use up the less expensive cuts of pork. (Montana)   □It's hard to find outstanding pork recipes—this is a family favorite. I add extra peppers and onions and serve it at least once a week. (Indiana)

SWEET-SOUR PORK

1½ lbs. boneless lean pork shoulder
½ tsp. salt
1 tblsp. cooking oil
¾ c. water
1 (13½ oz.) can pineapple chunks
3 tblsp. brown sugar, firmly packed
¼ tsp. ground ginger
3 tblsp. cornstarch
¼ c. cider vinegar
2 tblsp. soy sauce
1 medium green pepper, cut in 2-inch
   strips
1 medium onion, cut in thin slices
Hot fluffy rice

Cut pork into 2x½-inch strips. Sprinkle with salt. Brown pork in hot oil in 12-inch skillet. Add water. Bring to boil; reduce heat. Cover and simmer 1 hour or until pork is tender.

Drain pineapple, reserving juice. Add enough water to juice to make 1¼ c. Combine 1¼ c. reserved pineapple liquid, brown sugar, ginger, cornstarch, vinegar and soy sauce in bowl. Gradually stir into meat mixture. Cook until slightly thickened. Add green pepper, onion and pineapple. Cover and simmer 5 minutes. Serve over rice. Makes 4 servings.

I'm famous for Scalloped Potatoes and Pork Chops. (Kansas) ☐This is a great dish to serve guests when I'm extra busy as I don't have to fuss with mashed potatoes. Just add a vegetable and salad—a meal fit for a king! (South Dakota) ☐This is my relax-and-forget-it meal. I fix a make-ahead molded vegetable salad and dinner is complete. (Minnesota) ☐There are five hungry men at our house who never tire of this dish. (Iowa)

SCALLOPED POTATOES WITH PORK CHOPS

6 pork chops, ½-inch thick
1 tblsp. cooking oil
5 c. sliced, pared potatoes
6 (1 oz.) slices process American
   cheese
1 tsp. salt
¼ tsp. pepper
½ c. chopped green onions
1 (10½ oz.) can condensed cream of
   celery soup
1¼ c. milk

Brown pork chops on one side in hot oil in skillet. Remove chops as they brown; reserve drippings.

Place half of potatoes in greased 13x9x2-inch baking pan. Top with cheese slices and then remaining potatoes. Place pork chops, browned side up, on potatoes. Sprinkle with salt and pepper.

Cook onions in pan drippings in skillet until tender, but do not brown. Add soup and milk. Heat; then pour over chops. Cover with aluminum foil.

Bake in 350° oven 1 hour. Remove cover and continue baking 30 minutes or until meat and vegetables are tender. Makes 6 servings.

For years I attempted to make crisp chicken like my mother's, without success until I tried Crusty Fried Chicken. I took my first batch to a church supper—I couldn't believe my chicken disappeared first! (Indiana)   □I prepare most of this recipe the day before I'm expecting guests—so easy to fix and then I sit back and listen to the compliments. (Iowa)   □The flavor of this chicken is unique and it's so crunchy. I double the recipe, freeze half and have another delicious meal waiting in the freezer. (Michigan)

CRUSTY FRIED CHICKEN

3 (3 lb.) broiler-fryers (use breasts,
  thighs and legs)
2 pkgs. garlic salad dressing mix
3 tblsp. flour
2 tsp. salt
¼ c. lemon juice
2 tblsp. soft butter or regular
  margarine
Cooking oil
1 c. milk
1½ c. pancake mix

Wipe chicken pieces with damp paper towels. Combine salad dressing mix, flour and salt in small bowl. Add lemon juice and butter; mix to a smooth paste. Brush chicken on all sides with paste. Stack in bowl; cover. Refrigerate overnight.

About 1½ hours before serving, heat ¼ to ½-inch oil in large skillet or Dutch oven.

Dip chicken in milk; then coat well with pancake mix. Shake off excess pancake mix. Lightly brown chicken on all sides in hot oil.

As chicken browns, place in shallow baking pan, one layer deep. Spoon half of remaining dipping milk over chicken. Cover with lid or aluminum foil.

Bake in 375° oven 30 minutes. Remove lid. Baste chicken with remaining dipping milk. Bake 20 to 30 more minutes or until tender. Makes 8 servings.

Chicken With Dressing is easy to fix for a crowd. I made up several recipes and tucked them in the freezer for our 25th anniversary supper. Served with a molded vegetable salad, it was one of the most successful dinner menus I've ever had. Good plain food with a special touch. (Nebraska)   □When my sons and daughters come for dinner they always want Mom's good Chicken With Dressing. (Iowa)

CHICKEN WITH DRESSING

1 (3 to 4 lb.) stewing chicken, cut up
1 branch celery
1 onion, sliced
2 tsp. salt
3 peppercorns
¼ c. minced onion
⅓ c. butter or regular margarine
1½ qts. dry bread cubes
½ tsp. rubbed sage
½ tsp. salt
⅛ tsp. pepper
¾ c. flour
1½ tsp. salt
4 egg yolks, well beaten

Place chicken, celery, sliced onion, 2 tsp. salt and peppercorns in water to cover in kettle. Simmer, covered, 2 hours or until tender. Remove chicken from broth; cool. Reserve broth. Remove meat from bones; cut up. Arrange chicken in 3-qt. casserole.

Saute minced onion in melted butter in skillet. Combine onion, bread cubes, sage, ½ tsp. salt and ⅛ tsp. pepper; mix lightly. Sprinkle over chicken.

Skim fat from reserved broth. Reserve ½ c. fat. Strain broth; reserve 4 c. Heat reserved ½ c. fat in skillet. Stir in flour and 1½ tsp. salt. Blend in reserved broth. Cook, stirring constantly, until thickened. Add some hot mixture to yolks; stir back into hot mixture. Cook 1 minute. Pour over casserole.

Bake in 375° oven 35 minutes or until custard is set and golden brown on top. Makes 8 servings.

Chicken-Rice Bake can be fixed and popped in the oven—my kind of recipe. I toss a salad and serve homemade rolls from my freezer—everyone thinks I've worked for hours. (Indiana) □An ideal recipe to serve large groups, buffet style. It requires a minimum of fuss. I have given the recipe to many friends. (Pennsylvania) □A great inexpensive dish. We dry our own vegetables to add to this recipe. (Oregon) □Whenever I ask my family what shall we have for Sunday dinner—they all reply in a chorus: Chicken-Rice Bake. It's our favorite after-church dinner. (Kansas)

CHICKEN-RICE BAKE

1½ c. regular rice
1 (10¾ oz.) can condensed cream of
   mushroom soup
1 (10¾ oz.) can condensed
   cream of chicken soup
1 (10¾ oz.) can condensed
   cream of celery soup
1¾ c. milk
1 (3 to 4 lb.) broiler-fryer, cut up
1 (1⅜ oz.) pkg. onion soup mix

Arrange rice in greased 13x9x2-inch baking pan. Combine mushroom soup, chicken soup and celery soup in large saucepan. Gradually stir in milk. Heat over medium heat. Pour over rice layer.

Arrange chicken over rice. Sprinkle with dry soup mix. Cover with aluminum foil.

Bake in 325° oven 2 hours or until chicken is tender. Makes 6 servings.

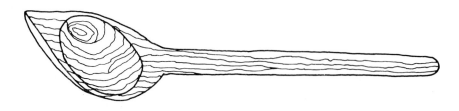

No matter how many times I make Paprika Chicken, my family never tires of it. It's easy to prepare and easy on the budget. The chicken is so tender, it melts in your mouth. (California) □I've tried so many recipes for chicken paprika but this one tops them all—it's outstanding. (Oklahoma) □My favorite buffet meal . . . I make it in an electric skillet and all help themselves. I always judge a recipe on how many requests I get for it—have lost track of how many times I have given this recipe to friends. (Ohio) □A company dish that's colorful, tastes great and doesn't cost a lot to make—but it looks elegant and special. We like it served with egg noodles. (Texas)

PAPRIKA CHICKEN

2 (2 lb.) broiler-fryers, cut up
⅓ c. flour
1 tblsp. paprika
¾ tsp. salt
⅛ tsp. pepper
⅓ c. cooking oil
½ c. chopped onion
3 chicken bouillon cubes
2½ to 3 c. hot water
1 c. dairy sour cream

Dredge chicken with mixture of flour, paprika, salt and pepper.

Brown chicken in hot oil in heavy skillet about 15 minutes. Add onion.

Dissolve bouillon cubes in hot water; add ½ c. to chicken in skillet. (Add more as needed.) Cover and simmer over low heat 30 to 40 minutes or until tender. Remove to serving platter.

Add remaining bouillon and sour cream to pan drippings. Stir well; heat. Makes 6 to 8 servings.

Summer Chicken with Peas—a beautiful all-in-one dish. (Utah) □This recipe turns out picture-perfect every time I make it. It's a thrill to make it and hear my guests rave and ask for the recipe. (California) □I have considered having several hundred copies of this recipe mimeographed, I've written the recipe down for so many friends. (Texas) □Even our minister who dislikes chicken looks forward to having this handsome meal at our home. When I invite him for dinner, he asks if we're having that tasty chicken dish. (Michigan)

SUMMER CHICKEN WITH PEAS

1 (2½ lb.) broiler-fryer, cut up
1 lb. new potatoes, scrubbed with a
   strip peeled around the center
6 tblsp. butter or regular margarine
Salt
Freshly ground pepper
2 tblsp. lemon juice
3 green onions, thinly sliced
1 lb. fresh peas, shelled (1 c.) or
   1 (10 oz.) pkg. frozen peas
¼ c. chopped fresh parsley
1 c. dairy sour cream
1 tsp. thyme leaves
½ tsp. salt
¼ tsp. pepper

Brown chicken and potatoes slowly on all sides in melted butter in large skillet. Season with salt and pepper. Sprinkle chicken with lemon juice. Reduce heat; cover and simmer 30 minutes.

Add green onions to butter in bottom of skillet. Sprinkle peas and parsley over chicken and potatoes; cover again and simmer 10 more minutes or until tender.

Remove chicken and vegetables to platter; keep warm. Remove skillet from heat. Pour off excess fat. Add sour cream, thyme, ½ tsp. salt and ¼ tsp. pepper. Stir to loosen pan drippings. Heat over low heat. Pour over chicken. Makes 4 servings.

American-Style Enchiladas—recipe, page 32

Summer Chicken with Peas—recipe, page 44

45

If you love dumplings, you simply must make Chicken with Dumplings. (Iowa)   □A delicious easy-to-fix cold weather dish. It's inexpensive and goes a long way. (Rhode Island)   □My family asks for this dish over and over again in the wintertime. I make extra gravy and add chunks of carrots. (Vermont)   □An old-time favorite with modern directions and ingredients—an easy and excellent recipe for good hearty appetites. (North Carolina)   □I've always had trouble with dumplings, either too soggy or tough. This recipe turns out beautifully every time. My family asks for this dish at least once a week. (Arizona)

CHICKEN WITH DUMPLINGS

1 (5 lb.) stewing chicken, cut up
1 branch celery
2 carrots, pared and sliced
1 onion, sliced
2 tsp. salt
1 qt. water
1 c. milk
⅓ c. flour
Parsley Dumplings (recipe follows)

Place chicken, celery, carrots, onion, salt and water in Dutch oven. Simmer, covered, 2½ to 3 hours or until chicken is tender.

Remove chicken from broth. Cool well. Remove meat from bones; cut in large pieces. Discard bones.

Strain broth and add enough water to make 3 c. Return broth to Dutch oven. Combine milk and flour in small jar. Cover and shake until smooth. Slowly stir into hot broth. Cook, stirring constantly, 5 minutes. Add chicken to gravy.

Prepare Parsley Dumplings. Makes 8 servings.

PARSLEY DUMPLINGS

2 c. sifted flour
3 tsp. baking powder
1 tsp. salt
¼ c. minced fresh parsley
¼ c. shortening
1 c. milk

Sift together flour, baking powder and salt into bowl. Mix in parsley. Cut in shortening with pastry blender until it looks like coarse cornmeal. Add milk; stir to make a soft dough. (Do not overmix.)

Drop dumpling mixture by spoonfuls onto simmering chicken gravy. Simmer, uncovered, 10 minutes. Cover and simmer 10 more minutes. Serve at once.

We have lots of stewing hens as we operate a poultry farm and Maine Chicken Pie gets fixed many times a month. My grandfather always has a third helping—he says it tastes just like the chicken pie his mother used to make on the farm years ago. (New Hampshire)   □A dish that tastes great fresh or frozen and a wonderful comforting pie to take to a shut-in—tempts the appetite. (New York)   □I associate this recipe with cold blustery days; that's when my family really looks forward to it. One Christmas Eve this was the star of my buffet. I added noodles and peas to the filling—compliments galore. (Nebraska)

MAINE CHICKEN PIE

1 (5 lb.) stewing chicken
1 small onion
1 whole carrot
1 stalk celery, cut up
2 tsp. salt
1½ qts. water
½ c. flour
½ tsp. onion salt
½ tsp. celery salt
⅛ tsp. pepper
2 or 3 drops yellow food color
Pastry for 2-crust 9-inch pie

Place chicken, onion, carrot, celery, salt and water in Dutch oven. Simmer, covered, 3 to 3½ hours or until tender. Remove chicken from broth; reserve 3½ c. broth. Cool chicken. Remove meat from bones; cut up.

Combine flour, onion salt, celery salt and pepper with ½ c. of reserved broth in small jar. Cover and shake until smooth. Heat remaining 3 c. broth in Dutch oven to boiling. Add flour mixture, stirring constantly, cook until thickened. Add food color and chicken; heat.

Pour mixture into pastry-lined pie plate. Cover with pastry. Seal and flute edges. Cut slits.

Bake in 400° oven 45 minutes or until golden brown. Makes 6 to 8 servings.

Crisp Oven-Fried Chicken requires no watching—and the pan drippings are so good spooned over mashed potatoes. (North Carolina)   □My friends think I should open a restaurant and serve only this fried chicken and French fries. They think people would come for miles to eat it. I agree. (Kansas)   □Our favorite way of serving chicken—I just put it in the oven, set the timer and forget about it—turns out so crispy and tender. (Pennsylvania)

CRISP OVEN-FRIED CHICKEN

1 c. crushed saltine crackers
¼ c. grated Parmesan cheese
1 tblsp. minced fresh parsley
½ tsp. salt
½ tsp. oregano leaves
½ tsp. basil leaves
½ tsp. celery salt
½ tsp. onion salt
¼ tsp. paprika
¼ tsp. pepper
½ bay leaf, crushed
2 (3 lb.) broiler-fryers, cut up
½ c. evaporated milk
⅓ c. cooking oil

Combine saltine crackers, Parmesan cheese, parsley, salt, oregano, basil, celery and onion salt, paprika, pepper and bay leaf in bowl. Dip chicken pieces in evaporated milk and then coat with crumb mixture. Place chicken in shallow roasting pan, skin side up.

Bake in 375° oven 30 minutes. Brush with oil; continue baking 30 more minutes or until golden brown and tender. Makes 8 servings.

My youngsters reject new dishes but when I made Salmon Loaf with Shrimp Sauce they tried it and asked for seconds. (New York)   □This is the only way my family will eat salmon. I make it often for supper, along with scalloped potatoes and beans. (Pennsylvania)   □Such a delicious way to stretch a can of salmon. The addition of green parsley makes it different and the sauce adds a special touch. (Ohio)

SALMON LOAF WITH SHRIMP SAUCE

2 (1 lb.) cans salmon
¼ c. finely minced onion
¼ c. chopped fresh parsley
¼ c. lemon juice
½ tsp. salt
½ tsp. pepper
½ tsp. thyme leaves
2 c. coarse cracker crumbs
Milk
4 eggs, well beaten
¼ c. melted butter or regular
   margarine
1 (10½ oz.) can condensed cream of
   shrimp soup
¼ c. milk

Drain salmon, reserving liquid. Flake salmon in bowl. Add onion, parsley, lemon juice, salt, pepper, thyme and cracker crumbs. Mix lightly.

Add enough milk to reserved liquid to make 1 c. Add liquid, eggs and butter to salmon; mix lightly. Spoon mixture into greased 8¼x4½x3-inch glass loaf baking dish.

Bake in 350° oven 1 hour or until loaf is set in center. Remove from baking dish onto serving platter. Combine soup and ¼ c. milk in saucepan; heat well. Serve with loaf. Makes 8 servings.

VEGETABLES

VEGETABLES

PLANTATION STUFFED PEPPERS
REFRIGERATOR MASHED POTATOES
WESTERN BAKED BEANS
CREOLE ZUCCHINI
MIXED VEGETABLES ITALIENNE
RATATOUILLE
BROCCOLI-RICE BAKE
INDIANA BAKED BEANS
BROCCOLI SOUFFLE
BARBECUED LIMA BEANS
SQUASH MEDLEY
STONE JAR SAUERKRAUT
CORN WITH CREAM CHEESE
BAKED STUFFED ZUCCHINI
ITALIAN ZUCCHINI
RANCHO BEANS
EGGPLANT PARMIGIANA

Vegetables Voted Extra-Special

Will it surprise you to read that six recipes using zucchini were selected as tops in the vegetable category? For years we've heard from women how their families just didn't like zucchini . . . that it was something of a problem, since their gardens produced a surplus from even a few plants.

In fact, reader complaints had prompted us to search out the best ways we could find to use this prolific summer squash. In our more recent cookbooks, we published a number of zucchini recipes. Our FARM JOURNAL recipes must have solved the surplus zucchini problem! Mothers sound almost joyous as they explain their children like zucchini "fixed this way." Baked Stuffed Zucchini, Italian Zucchini and Ratatouille all made a hit with adults, too. Husbands and field crews who insisted they didn't like zucchini now pass their plates for seconds when they are served any of these zucchini dishes.

Judging from cookbook users' comments, everyone likes baked beans. With bean recipes, the only problem seems to be making enough, especially for church suppers and picnics. Women describe baking Western Baked Beans, Barbecued Limas and Rancho Beans in huge roasting pans to serve a crowd. Busy women also treasure recipes that save time—and they singled out a potato recipe we think is one of our best. Refrigerator Mashed Potatoes, whipped with cream cheese and sour cream, will hold in the refrigerator for up to two weeks, ready anytime for heating in the oven. Corn with Cream Cheese is another favorite. Broccoli Souffle is a popular time-saver for company menus, as it can be made ahead and frozen.

Underlying all the comments, one senses a mother's concern that her family eat enough vegetables . . . and her pride and resourcefulness in fixing vegetables in imaginative ways. These are not all simple recipes! But they're so good and so popular with both men and children that women gladly invest their time.

When a vegetable hater reaches for seconds, you can be sure Mom marks that recipe for repeating. The great variety of vegetable recipes in this chapter have that kind of status in countless American homes today.

My kids love Plantation Stuffed Peppers. We harvest lots of peppers from our garden, but stuffed peppers were never popular with the family until I adopted your recipe. (Oregon)   □My family likes peppers fixed any way—but we all agree that these stuffed peppers are the tastiest of any recipe I have made. (Pennsylvania)   □My husband asks me to make these stuffed peppers often. I sometimes make the filling only and dice the green peppers to put into the mixture. Then I heat and serve over homemade onion rolls for a quick supper. (California)

PLANTATION STUFFED PEPPERS

1 lb. ground beef
1 c. chopped onion
1 clove garlic, minced
2 tsp. chili powder
½ tsp. salt
½ tsp. pepper
2 (10¾ oz.) cans condensed
   tomato soup
½ lb. sharp process cheese,
   shredded
1½ c. cooked parboiled rice
8 medium green peppers

Cook ground beef, onion and garlic in 10-inch skillet until is browned. Add chili powder, salt, pepper and tomato soup; simmer, covered, 10 minutes. Add cheese and rice; heat until cheese melts. Cool.

Cut peppers in halves lengthwise. Remove membranes and seeds. Cook in boiling salted water in Dutch oven until barely tender, about 3 minutes. Drain and cool. Place peppers on baking sheet. Spoon rice mixture into peppers. Place in freezer until frozen. Remove; wrap and label. Return to freezer. Recommended storage time: 3 months.

To serve: Place partially thawed peppers on baking sheet. Cover with aluminum foil. Bake in 400° oven 45 minutes or until hot. Makes 8 servings.

Refrigerator Mashed Potatoes—a make-ahead recipe that makes potatoes taste like a million. (Michigan) □This recipe is a super timesaver. The finished dish is delicious—tastes just like stuffed potatoes. Great to heat in a baking dish topped with lots of grated cheese. I cook for hired men every day except Sunday and this dish saves lots of pot washing. The men tell me that it's the best potato dish they ever tasted. (Colorado) □I have adapted this recipe to serve 100 for the Thanksgiving Lions Club Dinner—tastes ever so much better than plain mashed potatoes. (Indiana) □We have large family get-togethers on all holidays. I make your recipe for Refrigerator Mashed Potatoes 10 days ahead and then on the big day I just heat it in the oven. (Michigan)

REFRIGERATOR MASHED POTATOES

5 lbs. potatoes, pared and quartered
  (9 large)
2 (3 oz.) pkgs. cream cheese
1 c. dairy sour cream
2 tsp. onion salt
1 tsp. salt
¼ tsp. pepper
2 tblsp. butter or regular margarine

Cook potatoes in boiling salted water in Dutch oven until tender. Drain well.

Mash until smooth with potato masher. Add cream cheese, sour cream, onion salt, salt, pepper and butter. Beat with whisk or potato masher until smooth and fluffy. Place in refrigerator container. Cool and cover. Recommended storage time: 2 weeks.

To serve: Place desired amount of potatoes in greased casserole. Dot with butter and bake in 350° oven 30 minutes or until heated through. If you use full amount, heat in 2-qt. casserole. Makes 8 cups.

When I am planning to entertain a large group, I turn to your recipe for Western Baked Beans. It's also my contribution to potlucks and picnics—people look forward to it every year at our annual Sunday School picnic. (New York) □I was very honored when a friend's daughter called and asked me for the recipe for Western Beans. She planned to include them in her wedding buffet supper. (Arkansas) □If I don't have lima beans on hand, I substitute garbanzos and they taste just as good—it's an excellent recipe. (Montana) □Western Baked Beans are so tasty and the recipe makes a large amount for a crowd. We serve these beans in big soup tureens at our church suppers, so they're now known as "those good beans in the soup tureen." (New York)

WESTERN BAKED BEANS

8 strips bacon
4 large onions, sliced and
  separated in rings
½ to 1 c. brown sugar, firmly packed
1 tsp. dry mustard
½ tsp. garlic powder
1 tsp. salt
½ c. cider vinegar
2 (15 oz.) cans dried lima beans,
  drained
1 (1 lb.) can green lima beans, drained
1 (1 lb.) can dark red kidney
  beans, drained
1 (1 lb. 11 oz.) jar New England-style
  baked beans

Fry bacon in skillet until crisp. Drain on paper towels and crumble. Set aside.

Place onion rings in large skillet and add sugar, mustard, garlic powder, salt and vinegar. Cover and cook 20 minutes. Add onion mixture and bacon to the beans. Pour into 3-qt. casserole. Cover.

Bake in 350° oven 30 minutes. Uncover; bake 30 minutes more. Makes 12 servings.

My family had never tried zucchini until I found your recipe for Creole Zucchini. Now it ranks top choice with them. I add whole kernel corn to the recipe for taste and additional color. (California)   □This dish gives real zip to bland zucchini. It's a holiday favorite at Christmastime as I always freeze several batches of this tasty vegetable. It took years for my family to eat zucchini in any form. Your recipe did the job—it's the only zucchini recipe they will even consider eating. (Pennsylvania)   □A well-balanced and inexpensive dish because most of the ingredients come from our garden. (Illinois)

CREOLE ZUCCHINI

1 c. chopped onion
1 clove garlic, minced
¾ c. chopped green pepper
¼ c. cooking oil
2 lbs. zucchini, sliced (4 medium)
4 medium tomatoes, chopped
1½ tsp. salt
¼ tsp. pepper
¼ c. chopped fresh parsley
¼ c. grated Parmesan cheese

Cook onion, garlic and green pepper in hot oil in skillet until soft. Add zucchini, tomatoes, salt and pepper. Cover; cook over medium heat 20 minutes or until zucchini is tender. Serve topped with parsley and Parmesan cheese. Makes 8 servings.

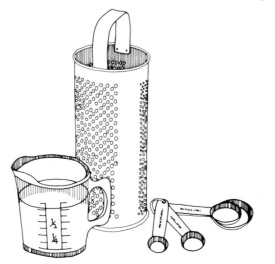

Mixed Vegetables Italienne is a scrumptious combination of end-of-summer vegetables from the garden—my family's favorite vegetable. (Washington)   □I make this at least once a week in my pressure cooker during the fresh vegetable season. It's a great meatless but nourishing meal that makes a hit with the entire family. (Connecticut)   □I like this recipe for its simplicity and good taste. It's a marvelous way to get the kids to eat all those different kinds of vegetables. (Ohio)   □This is such an easy, quick and delicious way to fix vegetables. I made this last summer for a big family reunion dinner. Everyone ate it with relish and several commented that they usually didn't eat those vegetables! (Oregon)

MIXED VEGETABLES ITALIENNE

¼ c. cooking oil
1 (1 lb.) can stewed tomatoes
1 beef bouillon cube
4 c. cubed zucchini (1-inch)
1½ c. cut-up green pepper (1-inch pieces)
1 c. frozen peas
1 c. frozen whole kernel corn
1 c. sliced pared carrots
1 c. diced pared potatoes
1 c. coarsely chopped onion
1 tsp. oregano leaves
1½ tsp. salt
⅛ tsp. pepper

Place all ingredients in 10-inch skillet. Cover and simmer 25 to 30 minutes or until vegetables are tender-crisp. Makes 6 servings.

Pressure Pan: Place all ingredients in pressure cooker. Close cover securely. Place over high heat. Bring to 15 lbs. pressure, according to manufacturer's directions for your pressure cooker. When pressure is reached (control will begin to jiggle), reduce heat immediately and cook 2 minutes. Remove from heat. Reduce pressure instantly by placing cooker under running faucet or in pan of cold water.

Mixed Vegetables Italienne—recipe, page 58

Broccoli Souffle—recipe, page 64   59

I've made this recipe for Ratatouille so often that my cookbook automatically falls open to the page! (New York) □A magnificent way to use late summer vegetables. (Minnesota) □My family raves about this vegetable dish. I freeze cartons of this so we can enjoy it all through the winter months. (Indiana) □Whenever I take this to potluck suppers, I'm assured of lots of compliments as well as recipe requests. (Ohio) □We raise all the vegetables that are in this recipe in our garden, as well as fresh basil. My kids especially like this dish because they have helped plant and harvest all the vegetables—gives them a feeling of pride. (Texas)

RATATOUILLE

2 medium onions, sliced
2 cloves garlic, chopped
¼ c. cooking oil
2 small zucchini, cut in
   ½-inch slices
3 medium tomatoes, diced
1 small eggplant, peeled and
   cut in 1-inch cubes
1 large green pepper, cut in
   strips
2 tblsp. chopped fresh parsley
2 tsp. salt
½ tsp. basil leaves
⅛ tsp. pepper

Saute onions and garlic in hot oil in Dutch oven until tender (do not brown). Add remaining ingredients. Cover and cook 15 minutes. Uncover and continue cooking 40 minutes or until vegetables are tender and juice is thickened. Stir occasionally. Makes 8 servings.

Broccoli-Rice Bake swept through our area when extension home economists used it to demonstrate vegetable cookery. It's great for potlucks, buffet company meals and Christmas holidays. (Minnesota)   □A recipe that turns broccoli haters into broccoli lovers. Every guest who insists he or she dislikes broccoli always takes home the recipe after tasting it at my house. (Connecticut)   □This recipe is the star of my favorite company menu. It's fast, and can be made ahead and frozen. (Maryland)   □I am always looking for new ways with vegetables. Broccoli-Rice Bake is my pet recipe. Great for parties; everyone raves about it. And it's so easy to make. (Kansas)

BROCCOLI-RICE BAKE

½ c. chopped celery
½ c. chopped onion
½ c. butter or regular margarine
1 (10¾ oz.) can condensed
   cream of mushroom soup
½ c. water
1 (8 oz.) jar pasteurized process
   cheese spread
1 (10 oz.) pkg. frozen chopped
   broccoli, thawed
1 (7 oz.) pkg. precooked rice

Saute celery and onion in melted butter in saucepan until tender (do not brown).

Combine soup, water and cheese spread. Add to saucepan. Heat until cheese melts. Add broccoli.

Cook rice according to package directions. Combine hot cheese mixture with cooked rice. Turn into greased 2-qt. casserole.

Bake in 350° oven 45 minutes or until hot. Makes 6 servings.

I wouldn't dare show up at our family reunions without Indiana Baked Beans. I always triple the recipe and add two chopped green peppers. (Nebraska) ☐We are a large family and there is usually one member who doesn't like one of the dishes I fix for dinner. These baked beans are the exception—everyone loves them. (Washington) ☐Every time our church has a supper, I am asked to bring "those good beans." (Wyoming) ☐Instead of using navy beans, I substitute pinto beans. The more this dish is reheated, the better it tastes. (Wisconsin)

INDIANA BAKED BEANS

4 lbs. dried beans (navy or pea)
4 qts. water
1 c. brown sugar, firmly packed
2 tblsp. salt
3½ tsp. prepared mustard
2 c. ketchup
1 c. molasses
1½ c. chopped onion
¾ lb. salt pork, sliced

Wash beans. Soak beans in water in large kettle overnight. (Or combine beans and water in large kettle. Bring to boiling; boil 2 minutes. Remove from heat. Cover and let stand 1 hour.) Do not drain.

Cover and simmer beans 1 hour or until almost tender. Add brown sugar, salt, mustard, ketchup, molasses and onion; bring to a boil. Pour beans into casseroles or bean pots. Mix some salt pork into beans; place remaining salt pork on top. Cover.

Bake in 300° oven 5 hours. Add boiling water during cooking to keep beans from becoming dry. Remove from oven. Pack in containers. Seal and freeze. Recommended storage time: 4 to 6 months.

To serve: Partially thaw at room temperature 2 hours. Heat beans with a little water in saucepan. Or bake in 350° oven 45 minutes for pints and 1 hour for quarts. Add water if necessary during heating.

There's always a Broccoli Souffle in my freezer, ready to pop into the oven and serve guests. (California)   □Our family likes the cheesy-onion flavor and colorful appearance; I like to keep a souffle in my freezer ready to bake for a buffet supper. Our favorite go-alongs are roast beef and potato puffs—a meal fit for a king, my husband tells me. (Iowa)   □Broccoli Souffle is so versatile—I have served it for a luncheon or as an unusual vegetable for company dinner. Have never had a failure—it always puffs up beautifully. (Oregon)

BROCCOLI SOUFFLE

3 tblsp. butter or regular margarine
3 tblsp. flour
1 c. milk
¼ tsp. salt
⅛ tsp. pepper
½ lb. American cheese, shredded (2 c.)
1 (10 oz.) pkg. frozen chopped
   broccoli, thawed
½ c. finely chopped onion
3 egg yolks, beaten
3 egg whites, stiffly beaten

Melt butter in saucepan; stir in flour. Add milk, salt and pepper; cook, stirring constantly, 5 minutes. Add cheese; stir until melted. Fold in broccoli, onion and egg yolks. Gently fold in egg whites. Pour into 2-qt. souffle dish. Set in shallow baking pan. Add hot water to pan to ½-inch depth.

Bake in 350° oven 1 hour or until puffy. Makes 6 to 8 servings.

Note: Unbaked souffle can be frozen. Pour mixture into foil-lined 2-qt. souffle dish. Cover and freeze.

When frozen, remove from dish. Wrap completely with aluminum foil; return to freezer. To serve frozen souffle: Remove foil. Place in souffle dish. Set in shallow baking pan. Add hot water to pan to ½-inch depth. Cover with foil. Bake in 350° oven 45 minutes. Remove foil. Bake 1 more hour or until puffy.

I come from a family of 12 adults. Whenever we gather together, I know I had better appear with a big casserole of Barbecued Lima Beans—or else! The standard greeting from some of my brothers is not "hello" but rather "Did you bring the beans?" I consider that a big compliment. (Nebraska) □I make this dish using four pounds of beans. Then I freeze half to serve during the busy harvest season as I know the men look forward to this hearty dish. (Kansas) □This is our favorite church supper bean recipe—we bake roasting pans full and still run out. (Pennsylvania)

BARBECUED LIMA BEANS

1 lb. dried lima beans
4 c. water
1½ c. chopped onion
1 c. brown sugar, firmly packed
1 c. ketchup
⅔ c. dark corn syrup
1 tblsp. salt
1 tblsp. liquid smoke
9 drops Tabasco sauce
Bacon strips

Wash beans. Soak beans in water in Dutch oven overnight. Do not drain. Add onion; bring to a boil. Cover and simmer 30 minutes or until beans are almost tender.

Combine brown sugar, ketchup, corn syrup, salt, liquid smoke and Tabasco sauce in bowl; mix well. Stir into beans. Cool quickly and pack into containers. Seal and freeze. Recommended storage time: 6 months. Makes 9 cups.

To serve: Thaw at room temperature until beans can be removed from container. Place in baking pan or casserole. Cover and bake in 400° oven until beans can be pressed into shape of baking pan or casserole. Top with bacon strips. Bake, uncovered, until beans are hot and bubbly. (Each quart of beans requires 1 hour baking.)

A much-praised vegetable casserole is a perfect description of this recipe for Squash Medley. (Texas) □The bacon and cheese give a pleasant flavor contrast to the bland squash. In the summer I often make this in my electric skillet and use several types of summer squash. (Oregon) □This recipe is easy to increase for a crowd and always makes a hit—a big favorite with men, I have found. (Nevada) □Squash grows plentifully in our area but is not a favorite vegetable. Last summer I tripled the recipe for Squash Medley, using several kinds of squash and brought it as my contribution to a school pot-luck. Everyone tried it and then returned for more. My phone rang for three days with requests for the recipe. (Illinois)

SQUASH MEDLEY

4 fresh medium unpeeled summer
  squash, or 4 c. frozen summer
  squash
½ green pepper, chopped
3 medium ripe tomatoes, peeled and
  chopped
6 strips bacon, cooked, drained and
  crumbled
1½ c. shredded process cheese
⅓ c. chopped onion
½ tsp. salt
½ c. dry bread crumbs
2 tblsp. butter or regular margarine

Parboil squash in boiling water in saucepan (zucchini for 3 minutes; yellow crooknecks or small white pattypans, 5 minutes; and white scallops, 15 minutes. (If you use frozen squash, do not parboil.)

Combine green pepper, tomatoes, bacon, cheese, onion, salt and pepper in bowl; mix well. Slice parboiled squash thinly. Place in baking dish, alternating squash and filling. Top with bread crumbs and dot with butter.

Bake in 375° oven 35 minutes or until hot. Makes 6 to 8 servings.

The recipe for Stone Jar Sauerkraut makes such a good kraut, with easy-to-follow directions. I make this recipe for my family, friends and the county fair—everyone rates it a winner. (Colorado)   □I have made many sauerkraut recipes over the years, sometimes with great success and other times just a so-so product. Since I have been making Stone Jar Sauerkraut, I have perfect results every time. (Illinois)   □This recipe for sauerkraut is so simple to make. The recipe explains each step so well that you couldn't possibly make a mistake. (Illinois)

STONE JAR SAUERKRAUT

You will need roughly 5 lbs. cabbage for every gallon of your crock. For instance, a 10-gallon crock would need about 50 lbs. of cabbage.

Quarter cabbage and shred finely. Place 5 lbs. shredded cabbage and 3½ tblsp. pickling salt in large pan. Mix well with hands. Pack gently in clean scalded crock, using a potato masher to press it down. Repeat above procedure until crock is filled to within 5 inches from the top.

Press cabbage down firmly with potato masher to extract enough juice to cover. Cover with clean cloth. Place a plate on top and weight it down with a jar filled with water.

Keep crock at 65° to ferment. Check kraut daily. Remove scum as it forms. Wash and scald cloth often to keep it free from scum and mold. Fermentation will be complete in 10 to 12 days. (If no bubbles rise, fermentation has ended.)

Pack in hot jars to within 1-inch from top. Add enough juice to cover. If you need more juice, make a weak brine by combining 2 tblsp. salt and 1 qt. water. Cover; screw band tight. Process in boiling water bath 15 minutes for pints; 20 minutes for quarts. Fifty pounds of cabbage makes 15 quarts.

Stone Jar Sauerkraut—recipe, page 68

Corn with Cream Cheese makes canned corn taste extra-special. And it only takes minutes to prepare. My family likes this so well that I order corn by the case. We have it at least once a week. (Wisconsin)   □Whenever I fix this dish for company I know that someone will ask, "What makes this so deliciously rich and creamy?" It's one of the best and easiest ways to dress up corn that I have ever found. (Indiana)   □My family loves this corn recipe and guests do, too. It's a popular quantity recipe at our church suppers. The cream cheese gives the corn a completely different flavor—a gourmet dish with little effort. (Nebraska)

CORN WITH CREAM CHEESE

¼ c. milk
1 (3 oz.) pkg. cream cheese
1 tblsp. butter or regular
   margarine
½ tsp. salt
⅛ tsp. pepper
2 (12 oz.) cans whole kernel
   corn, drained (3 c.)

Combine milk, cream cheese, butter, salt and pepper in saucepan.

Cook over low heat, stirring constantly, until cheese melts and is blended. Add corn and heat. Makes 6 servings.

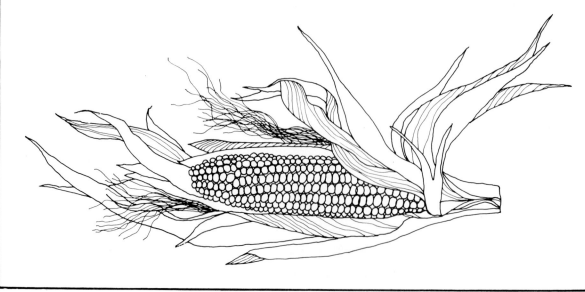

My children call Baked Stuffed Zucchini "that special squash dish." They always used to turn up their noses when I served squash. Now it's their favorite vegetable. My five-year-old insists she could eat this every day. (North Dakota) □This is one of my favorite summertime recipes. By using your basic recipe with my own variations, I can prepare dishes to freeze ahead for winter meals. Sometimes I substitute ground beef for part of the spinach and add several spices for a different treat. (New Mexico)

BAKED STUFFED ZUCCHINI

8 small to medium zucchini
2 medium onions
1 clove garlic
12 sprigs parsley
3 tblsp. cooking oil
1 c. Swiss chard or spinach,
  cooked and drained
1½ tsp. salt
1 tsp. oregano leaves
⅛ tsp. pepper
½ c. grated Parmesan cheese
3 eggs, beaten
⅔ c. dry bread crumbs

Cook zucchini in boiling water 5 minutes. Drain and cool. Cut in half lengthwise; scoop out centers leaving ¼-inch shell. Reserve pulp.

Chop onions, garlic and parsley in blender. Saute in hot oil in skillet. Chop reserved pulp and Swiss chard in blender; drain off excess liquid. Add to onions; saute a few minutes. Stir in salt, oregano, pepper, Parmesan cheese, eggs and bread crumbs; mix well. Place shells on baking sheet. Fill with mixture. Place in freezer until frozen. Remove and wrap in foil. Label; return to freezer. Recommended storage time: 2 months. Makes 16 servings.

To serve: Arrange frozen stuffed zucchini in baking pan. Cover and bake in 350° oven 45 minutes. Uncover and bake 10 more minutes.

I've found the best way to coax my family to eat zucchini, which is not their favorite vegetable, is to serve them Italian Zucchini. (Kansas) □"But I don't like zucchini," our hired man kept repeating as he demolished three helpings of this delicious Italian Zucchini. (Nebraska) □We always seem to have a surplus of zucchini from our garden and the family tires of it. But they never turn down Italian Zucchini because it tastes so good, they tell me. (Indiana) □A great recipe for family reunions. I usually triple the recipe and even then it's the first vegetable on the buffet to disappear. (Iowa)

ITALIAN ZUCCHINI

4 medium zucchini (about 2 lbs.)
¼ c. cooking oil
1½ c. chopped onion
1½ tsp. salt
¼ tsp. garlic salt
¼ tsp. pepper
⅛ tsp. oregano leaves
2 (1 lb. 12 oz.) cans tomatoes or
   3 c. chopped tomatoes

Remove ends from zucchini and discard. Cut in lengthwise halves. Cut each half in thirds crosswise. Place cut side down in hot oil in 12-inch skillet. Add onion. Cook until zucchini is lightly browned.

Sprinkle zucchini with salt, garlic salt, pepper and oregano. Top with tomatoes. Cover and simmer 15 minutes. Uncover and simmer 20 minutes or until squash is tender and a fairly thick sauce is formed. Makes 8 servings.

Rancho Beans is one of the few recipes that my husband asks me to make, especially during the cold weather months. (Michigan) □This bean recipe is so versatile. I've prepared it for family meals, camping, church functions and picnics. It's easy and tasty with or without the ground beef. (Maryland) □A quick and hearty meal and my gang loves it. It's one of my favorite microwave oven dishes. (New York) □A four-generation recipe in our family: my great-grandchildren tell me that this is their most favorite baked bean recipe. (New Mexico)

RANCHO BEANS

1 lb. lean ground beef
1 envelope dry onion soup mix
1 c. ketchup
2 tblsp. prepared mustard
½ c. water
2 tsp. cider vinegar
2 (1 lb.) cans pork and beans in
    tomato sauce
1 (1 lb.) can kidney beans

Brown ground beef in large skillet over medium heat. Add the remaining ingredients; mix well. Heat thoroughly. Pour into 3-qt. casserole.

Bake in 400° oven 30 minutes or until bubbling hot in center. Makes 8 to 10 servings.

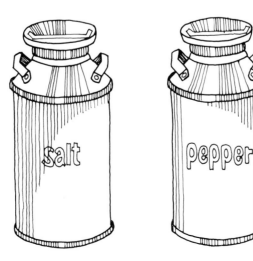

Even people who don't care for eggplant tell me they think that Eggplant Parmigiana is superb. (Michigan) □We have this FARM JOURNAL recipe often when eggplants are in season. Have tried many other recipes for this dish—yours is the greatest. (Maryland) □What a wonderful way to use up our bountiful crop of eggplants. Tastes so much better than batter-fried eggplant, which was my family's favorite until they tasted this dish. (Connecticut) □We grow all our own vegetables. When I want to make Eggplant Parmigiana, I gather the vegetables and in no time at all I am ready to serve this fresh-tasting dish from the bounty of our produce. (Iowa)

EGGPLANT PARMIGIANA

2 medium eggplants, pared and
   cut in ½-inch slices (2 lbs.)
½ c. flour
½ tsp. salt
⅛ tsp. pepper
¼ to ½ c. cooking oil
2 (8 oz.) cans tomato sauce
1 (8 oz.) pkg. mozzarella
   cheese, thinly sliced
½ c. grated Parmesan cheese

Sprinkle eggplant with salt. Spread out in layer on board or paper towels; let stand 20 minutes. Pat dry with paper towels.

Dip each slice in mixture of flour, ½ tsp. salt and pepper. Heat ¼ c. oil in 10-inch skillet. Brown eggplant quickly. (Cooking quickly over medium heat will keep eggplant from absorbing a lot of oil.) Drain on paper towels.

Pour ¼-inch tomato sauce in greased 2-qt. casserole. Top with one-third of eggplant slices, one-third of remaining tomato sauce and one-third of cheeses. Repeat layers twice. Cover.

Bake in 400° oven 20 minutes. Remove cover and continue baking 10 minutes. Makes 6 servings.

SALADS

SALADS

GLAZED FRUIT SALAD
CREAMY FROZEN SALAD
OVERNIGHT BEAN SALAD
CABBAGE-ONION SALAD
FROZEN FRUIT SALAD-DESSERT
RIBBON SALAD
THREE-ROW GARDEN SALAD
FROSTED CRANBERRY SALAD
OVERNIGHT TOSSED SALAD
SUN GOLD FRUIT SALAD
OVERNIGHT SALAD
BAKED GERMAN POTATO SALAD
STRAWBERRY SALAD
CUCUMBER-SOUR CREAM SALAD

Superior Salads

FARM JOURNAL cookbook users made it clear that family reunions, picnics and outdoor barbecues aren't complete without a salad. Many of the homemakers who selected a salad as top favorite were remembering the plaudits of family and neighbors—take one of these salads to a community gathering, they say, and your reputation as a good cook will be secure. Each voter was proud to tell us that the FARM JOURNAL recipe she had adopted was considered outstanding—that the family gathering wouldn't be the same without it. In fact, many women told us that when they arrived at the yearly family reunion, the first greeting was not "How are you?" but "Did you bring that good salad?" Overnight Bean Salad and Glazed Fruit Salad are prominent in this category.

It's interesting that all the salads the women voted for are make-ahead, no doubt a reason as important as good taste for their popularity. Make-ahead also suggests portability—a salad that can be carried out for community suppers or picnics. At home, it means that one part of the meal is all done—a steadying thought for any homemaker or hostess facing the last-minute rush to get dinner on the table. There's even an Overnight Tossed Salad which women tell us they've carried successfully to potlucks. The greens are covered with a layer of creamy mayonnaise to keep them crisp and fresh until serving time.

The voting also verified a country preference for fruit salads—or salad/desserts, as they're often served. But there are five good ways to serve vegetables in this collection.

Several "just like Mother used to make" salads, such as Baked German Potato Salad and Cucumber-Sour Cream Salad, showed up as favorites. FARM JOURNAL'S recipes came closest to their childhood memories, these partisans said.

Holiday entertaining calls for a very special salad in most homes, and farm women described several cherished FARM JOURNAL recipes, with Ribbon Salad and Frosted Cranberry Salad the two top choices. They have become the traditional Christmas salad in many homes across the country. You'll have a hard time selecting your favorite from this collection.

Glazed Fruit Salad is an unusual and colorful salad. I have even served it as a breakfast fruit for a special treat to my family. (Minnesota) ☐We like this fruit salad because it's not overly rich and heavy as many creamy salads tend to be. I've served it for lunch, dinner and breakfast too, and it always goes over big with family and friends. (Iowa) ☐A good picnic salad as there is no gelatin that might melt on a hot summer day. It makes a big batch and even though I make a double recipe I never seem to have enough—everyone makes a beeline for this salad at our outdoor gatherings. (Kansas)

GLAZED FRUIT SALAD

1 (1 lb. 4 oz.) can pineapple chunks,
   well drained
1 (1 lb. 14 oz.) can fruit cocktail,
   well drained
2 (11 oz.) cans mandarin orange
   segments, well drained
7 or 8 bananas, sliced
2 tblsp. lemon juice
1 (1 lb. 6 oz.) can apricot or peach
   pie filling
Lettuce

Combine pineapple chunks, fruit cocktail and mandarin oranges in large bowl. Add bananas, lemon juice and apricot pie filling; mix gently. Cover and chill several hours or overnight. Serve in lettuce cups. Makes 12 servings.

The simplicity of Creamy Frozen Salad appeals to me. I have never seen this in any other cookbook. It's a great success wherever I take it and tastes so good with any meal. (Indiana) □This recipe is so handy to have in the freezer. When I don't have time to make a salad for dinner, I count on having this waiting in the freezer. We like it for dessert, too. I freeze it in cupcake liners for company dinners. (Missouri) □Every time I make this salad, I triple the recipe—and it still disappears rapidly. But, I never run out, because I always make sure there is a batch in the freezer at all times. (Virginia)

CREAMY FROZEN SALAD

2 c. dairy sour cream
2 tblsp. lemon juice
¾ c. sugar
⅛ tsp. salt
1 (8½ oz.) can crushed
      pineapple, drained
¼ c. sliced maraschino cherries
¼ c. chopped pecans
1 medium banana, sliced

Blend together sour cream, lemon juice, sugar and salt in bowl. Stir in pineapple, maraschino cherries, pecans and banana.

Pour into 1-qt. mold or paper-lined muffin-pan cups. Cover and freeze. Let thaw at room temperature 15 minutes before serving. Makes 8 servings.

Everyone loves Overnight Bean Salad at our house—from the youngest to the oldest—our great-grandfather. (Indiana) ☐Of all the recipes I have, your Overnight Bean Salad is the one that I receive the most requests for. It's a picnic favorite and my husband likes it in his lunchbox. We like it made with tarragon vinegar. (Ohio)   ☐This is what I call a please-make-this-soon-Mom recipe. I like it, too, because I can make it ahead to use during a busy period and it tastes better the longer it stands. (Illinois)   ☐I often take this to a family that has had a crisis. Many people tend to bring sweets and desserts so this tangy vegetable salad is always welcome. (Wyoming)

OVERNIGHT BEAN SALAD

1 (1 lb.) can French-cut green
   beans, drained
1 (1 lb.) can wax beans, drained
1 (1 lb.) can kidney beans, drained
½ c. chopped green pepper
½ c. chopped onion
½ c. salad oil
½ c. vinegar
¾ c. sugar
1 tsp. salt
½ tsp. pepper
Lettuce

Combine green beans, wax beans, kidney beans, green pepper and onion in bowl. Combine oil, vinegar, sugar, salt and pepper in jar. Cover and shake well. Pour over bean mixture. Cover.

Chill in refrigerator overnight or at least 6 hours. Serve in lettuce cups. Makes 8 to 10 servings.

Cabbage-Onion Salad keeps well and tastes better every day—the kind of recipe I like. (Oklahoma) □I add green and red sweet peppers equal to the amount of onion in the recipe—wonderful flavor and texture. (South Dakota) □I use this recipe year round for family dinners, camping trips, community suppers and to please my in-laws who always want me to make it when they come to visit. (Montana) □A colorful, big salad that's a perfect go-along with baked ham and scalloped potatoes—a favorite winter dinner with us. (Minnesota)

CABBAGE-ONION SALAD

8 c. shredded cabbage
  (1 large head)
2 large onions, thinly sliced and
  separated in rings
1 c. sugar
1 c. vinegar
1 tsp. salt
1 tsp. celery seeds
1 tsp. dry mustard
¼ tsp. pepper
1 c. salad oil

Alternate layers of cabbage and onions in bowl, ending with onions.

Combine sugar, vinegar, salt, celery seeds, mustard and pepper in 2-qt. saucepan. Bring to a boil. Remove from heat; add salad oil.

Drip the hot mixture over cabbage and onions; do not stir. Cover and refrigerate 24 hours or longer before serving. Toss salad before serving. Makes about 8 cups.

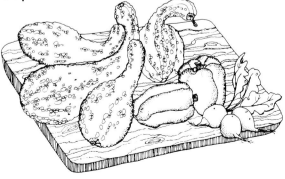

I remember having Frozen Fruit Salad-Dessert as a child on the farm 50 years ago. After years of searching for a recipe, I finally found it in your first cookbook. It tasted just like my mother's salad . . . now I always have a batch in the freezer. (Idaho)   □This is by far the very best frozen salad I have ever eaten. And so good for big groups. We freeze it in small cupcake papers and get more than 60 servings for our annual church Christmas Party. (New York)   □Friends have called me long distance for this recipe—so good to have on hand for the busy farm seasons and the holidays. The youngsters like it as an after-school snack—it's not too sweet. (West Virginia)

FROZEN FRUIT SALAD-DESSERT

4 (1 lb. 4 oz.) cans crushed pineapple
2 (1 lb.) cans sliced peaches, drained
1 env. unflavored gelatin
¼ c. cold water
1 c. orange juice
¼ c. lemon juice
2½ c. sugar
½ tsp. salt
2 c. halved green seedless grapes
1½ c. cut-up maraschino cherries
30 marshmallows, quartered (½ lb.)
2 tsp. finely chopped crystallized
    ginger
2 c. coarsely chopped pecans
2 qts. heavy cream, whipped
3 c. mayonnaise

Drain pineapple, reserving 1½ c. juice. Cut peaches in ½-inch cubes. Set aside.

Soften gelatin in cold water 5 minutes. Heat 1½ c. juice in saucepan. Bring to boiling; remove from heat. Add gelatin; stir to dissolve. Stir in orange and lemon juice, sugar and salt. Chill until it thickens.

Fold in all fruits, marshmallows, ginger, pecans, cream and mayonnaise. Spoon into 1-qt. cylinder containers. Cover and freeze. Thaw slightly before serving. Remove from container; cut into 1-inch slices. Makes 9 quarts or 72 servings.

Frozen Fruit Salad-Dessert—recipe, page 82

Three-Row Garden Salad—recipe, page 86

84   **Ribbon Salad—recipe, page 85**

I was so proud when I served your recipe for Ribbon Salad on Christmas Eve. Everyone thought it was beautiful. Although it is a large salad, it disappeared in a hurry. (Missouri) □This is my year-round salad for special occasions. It's a must at our Christmas dinner. For Valentine's Day, I make two red layers. And for Easter dinner to serve along with baked ham I use lemon and lime-flavored gelatin for spring-like flavor and color. (Idaho) □I just make the lemon-pineapple layer of the salad. We think it's a perfect accompaniment for New England baked beans—traditional in our home on Saturday night. (Maine)

RIBBON SALAD

2 (3 oz.) pkgs. lime flavor gelatin
5 c. boiling water
4 c. cold water
1 (1 lb. 4 oz.) can crushed pineapple
1 (3 oz.) pkg. lemon flavor gelatin
½ c. cut-up miniature marshmallows
1 (8 oz.) pkg. cream cheese
1 c. heavy cream, whipped
1 c. mayonnaise
2 (3 oz.) pkgs. cherry flavor gelatin

Dissolve lime gelatin in 2 c. of the boiling water in bowl. Stir in 2 c. of the cold water. Pour into 13x9x2-inch baking pan. Chill until partially set.

Drain pineapple, reserving 1 c. juice. Set aside.

Dissolve lemon gelatin in 1 c. boiling water in double boiler top. Add marshmallows; place over simmering water. Stir until marshmallows are melted. Remove from heat. Add 1 c. reserved juice and cream cheese. Beat with rotary beater until well blended. Stir in pineapple; cool. Fold in whipped cream and mayonnaise. Chill until thickened.

Pour over lime gelatin layer. Chill until almost set.

Dissolve cherry gelatin in remaining 2 c. boiling water in bowl. Stir in remaining 2 c. cold water. Chill until thick and syrupy. Pour over pineapple layer. Chill until set. Cut in squares. Makes 24 servings.

I keep a picture of your Three-Row Garden Salad pasted to the inside of my cupboard door. It's easy-to-fix, delicious, nutritious and receives raves from my guests. (Oregon) □The recipe for this salad speaks for itself—well worth the effort of preparation time. Looks and tastes so garden-fresh—this salad was the highlight of our Mother-Daughter Banquet. (New York) □A fun-to-fix salad that looks so pretty—and the vegetables come from our garden. (Nebraska)

THREE-ROW GARDEN SALAD

1 (3 oz.) pkg. orange flavor gelatin
1 c. boiling water
¾ c. pineapple juice
2 tblsp. lemon juice
1½ c. finely shredded carrots
1 (3 oz.) pkg. lime flavor gelatin
1 c. boiling water
¾ c. pineapple juice
2 tblsp. lemon juice
1½ c. grated cabbage
2 tsp. unflavored gelatin
½ c. cold water
1 (3 oz.) pkg. lemon flavor gelatin
½ tsp. salt
1 c. boiling water
2 tblsp. beet juice
2 tblsp. vinegar
1 c. finely diced cooked beets, well
   drained
1 tblsp. horseradish
Cheese-Horseradish Dressing
   (recipe follows)

Prepare layers separately, allowing about 15 minutes between each so that gelatins set at intervals.

To make orange layer, dissolve orange flavor gelatin in 1 c. boiling water. Add ¾ c. pineapple juice and 2 tblsp. lemon juice; chill until thick and syrupy. Fold in carrots.

To make green layer, dissolve lime flavor gelatin in 1 c. boiling water. Add ¾ c. pineapple juice and

2 tblsp. lemon juice; chill until thick and syrupy. Fold in cabbage.

To make red layer, soften unflavored gelatin in cold water. Dissolve lemon gelatin and salt in 1 c. boiling water; immediately stir in unflavored gelatin mixture. Add beet juice and vinegar; chill until thick and syrupy. Fold in beets and horseradish.

Layer gelatines—orange, green then red in 9x5x3-inch loaf pan. Allow each layer to set partially before adding second or third layer. Chill until set.

To unmold set pan in warm (not hot) water about 5 seconds; loosen around beet layer and turn out on platter. Prepare Horseradish Dressing and serve with salad. Makes 10 servings.

CHEESE-HORSERADISH DRESSING

1 (3 oz.) pkg. cream cheese, softened
¼ c. mayonnaise
2 tblsp. milk
½ tsp. celery salt
2 tsp. horseradish
2 tsp. chopped chives

Beat cream cheese in bowl until creamy. Blend in mayonnaise, milk, celery salt and horseradish. Fold in chives. Makes ¾ c.

I couldn't be without Frosted Cranberry Salad. It's my round-the-clock salad; I serve it for meals or snacks. It fits into so many situations and menus. (Georgia) □A very different and delicious salad. I double the recipe for club meetings and party buffets. I sometimes substitute pecans for walnuts, sour cream for heavy cream and use cherry gelatin in place of the raspberry. (Washington) □This is our traditional Thanksgiving and Christmas salad. (Nebraska) □I freeze this salad in individual tortoni cups and store in plastic bags in the freezer. (Iowa) □Whenever I serve turkey with dressing the family just knows they will have that yummy Cranberry Salad. (Michigan)

FROSTED CRANBERRY SALAD

1 (8½ oz.) can crushed pineapple
1 (1 lb.) can whole cranberry sauce
2 (3 oz.) pkgs. raspberry flavor
  gelatin
1 (8 oz.) pkg. cream cheese, softened
2 tblsp. salad dressing
1 c. heavy cream, whipped
½ c. coarsely chopped walnuts
1 tart apple, pared and chopped

Drain pineapple and cranberry sauce, reserving liquid. Add enough water to liquid to make 2 c. Pour 2 c. liquid into saucepan; bring to a boil. Remove from heat. Dissolve gelatin in hot liquid in bowl. Chill until partially set.

Beat together cream cheese and salad dressing in large bowl until fluffy. Gradually beat in gelatin. Fold mixture into whipped cream. Remove 1½ c. of mixture; let stand at room temperature.

Fold pineapple, cranberry sauce, walnuts and apple into remaining gelatin mixture. Pour into 11x7x1½-inch baking dish. Chill until surface sets, about 20 minutes.

Spread reserved topping on top. Chill several hours before serving. Makes 12 servings.

When my family tires of ordinary tossed salad, I whip up a batch of Overnight Tossed Salad—stays fresh and crisp for several meals. (Missouri) □A perfect salad to carry to potlucks. It can be prepared in advance and travels well. (South Dakota) □A wonderful combination of flavor and crunch. I sometimes substitute cauliflower for peas—the bowl passes around the table until every bit is gone. (Illinois)

OVERNIGHT TOSSED SALAD

6 c. chopped lettuce
½ tsp. salt
½ tsp. sugar
⅛ tsp. pepper
6 hard-cooked eggs, sliced
1 (10 oz.) pkg. frozen peas, thawed
½ lb. bacon, crisp-cooked and
   crumbled
½ c. sliced green onions and tops
½ c. sliced celery
2 c. shredded process Swiss cheese
  (8 oz.)
1¼ c. mayonnaise or salad dressing

Place half the lettuce in a large bowl. Sprinkle with salt, sugar and pepper. Top with layer of eggs, then peas, bacon, remaining lettuce, green onion, celery and cheese.

Spread mayonnaise evenly over the top to cover. Place tight cover on bowl and refrigerate 24 hours. Toss just before serving. Makes 8 servings as a main dish, 12 as a side dish in a meal.

The first time that I served this Sun Gold Fruit Salad with fluffy topping was to celebrate a family birthday dinner. It tasted so good and looked so pretty that it became my dinner-party salad. My guests say they have never seen such a handsome salad. (Wisconsin)   □We are partial to fruit salad and I especially like it because it can be made ahead. The topping puts it in the "company class". We always have it for our Thanksgiving salad. (Wisconsin)   □I've become famous at church picnics for my FARM JOURNAL great fruit salad. (New York)

SUN GOLD FRUIT SALAD

2 (3 oz.) pkgs. orange flavor gelatin
2 c. boiling water
1½ c. cold water
1 (11 oz.) can mandarin orange
   segments
1 (8¾ oz.) can apricot halves
1 c. seedless green grapes
2 large bananas, sliced
6 tblsp. sugar
2 tblsp. cornstarch
1 egg, slightly beaten
2 tblsp. butter or regular margarine
1 tblsp. lemon juice
1 c. heavy cream, whipped
¼ c. shredded Cheddar cheese

Dissolve gelatin in boiling water in bowl. Stir in cold water. Chill until thick and syrupy.

Drain mandarin orange segments and apricots, reserving 1 c. liquid. Fold mandarin orange segments, apricots, grapes and bananas into gelatin. Pour into 9x5x3-inch loaf pan. Chill overnight.

Combine sugar and cornstarch in small saucepan. Blend in egg and 1 c. reserved liquid. Cook over low heat, stirring constantly, until thickened. Remove from heat; stir in butter and lemon juice. Cool. Fold in whipped cream. Unmold gelatin. Frost with cream mixture. Sprinkle with cheese. Chill until topping sets. Makes 12 servings.

Overnight Salad is so-o-o-o good. It's become our tradition-al holiday salad. (Connecticut)   □The women from our church committee went wild over this salad, which I served for refreshment with coffee. So different from the cakes and cookies that are usually served. (Iowa)   □My family would rather have this salad for dessert than a heavy cake or pie. Even if you change or substitute fruits, as I often do, this salad is still superb—a quick and dependable recipe that I can whip up quickly for any occasion. (Washington)

OVERNIGHT SALAD

2 eggs
¼ c. white vinegar
¼ c. sugar
2 tblsp. butter or regular margarine
1 c. heavy cream, whipped
1 (1 lb. 4 oz.) can pineapple chunks,
    drained and cut in half
2 c. halved seedless green grapes
2 oranges, peeled and diced
2 c. miniature marshmallows

Beat eggs in double boiler top. Add vinegar, sugar and butter. Cook over simmering water, stirring constantly, until thickened. Remove from heat and cool well.

Fold cooled custard into whipped cream. Combine pineapple, grapes, oranges and marshmallows in large bowl. Pour whipped cream mixture overall; toss gently to mix. Cover and chill 24 hours. Makes 8 to 10 servings.

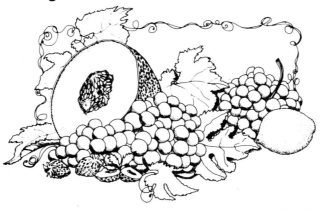

This Baked German Potato Salad tastes exactly like the delicious potato salad I remember as a young girl. In those days very few cooks used a recipe so it turned out differently each time. Your recipe comes the closest to my childhood memories. I add a bit more sugar and omit the radishes—we love it. (Michigan)   □Every time I entertain 15 or 20 people I make this potato salad. Even though I usually set out seven or eight different dishes, the potato salad disappears first. It's my standby for picnics, parties, potlucks, Christmas and Easter buffet dinners. (Illinois)   □This is such an easy recipe to make and it's not too spicy. (Ohio)

BAKED GERMAN POTATO SALAD

8 strips bacon, cubed
1 c. chopped celery
1 c. chopped onion
3 tblsp. flour
1⅓ c. water
1 c. cider vinegar
⅔ c. sugar
1 tsp. salt
¼ tsp. pepper
8 c. cubed cooked potatoes
    (about 8 medium)
1 c. sliced radishes (optional)

Fry bacon in 10-inch skillet until crisp. Remove and drain on paper towels. Drain off fat and measure. Return ¼ c. fat to skillet. Add celery and onion; cook 1 minute. Blend in flour. Then stir in water and vinegar; cook, stirring constantly, until mixture is thick and bubbly. Stir in sugar, salt and pepper. Pour mixture over potatoes and bacon in greased 3-qt. casserole. Mix lightly. Cover.

Bake in 350° oven 30 minutes. Remove from oven. Stir in radishes, if desired. Serve at once. Makes 10 to 12 servings.

I have made Strawberry Salad for several baby and wedding showers as well as for a Christmas buffet and for my husband's birthday (at his request)—it's a year-round delight. (Washington) □I have served this more than any other of my salad recipes except for a tossed green salad. It is the most popular salad at our afternoon women's meetings. (California) □I first tasted this salad at a friend's home during the holidays. Then I made it as a surprise for my mother's and sister's Fourth-of-July birthdays. I garnished it with whipped cream and fresh blueberries for a red, white and blue effect. (Arizona) □A favorite with me because it's so pretty, so easy and inexpensive to make for a company dessert. (Tennessee)

STRAWBERRY SALAD

2 (3 oz.) pkgs. strawberry flavor
  gelatin
2 c. boiling water
2 (10 oz.) pkgs. frozen strawberries
1 (1 lb. 4 oz.) can crushed pineapple
2 large bananas, mashed
1 c. dairy sour cream
1 (3 oz.) pkg. cream cheese
½ c. heavy cream, whipped
1 c. mayonnaise
Lettuce

Dissolve gelatin in boiling water in bowl. Add unthawed strawberries and stir until berries are separated. Add undrained pineapple and bananas; mix well. Pour half of gelatin mixture into 9-inch square baking pan. Chill until set. Let remaining gelatin mixture stand at room temperature.

Whip together sour cream and cream cheese in bowl. Spread over first gelatin layer. Top with remaining gelatin mixture. Chill until set.

Fold whipped cream into mayonnaise in small bowl. Cut salad in squares and place on lettuce. Top with mayonnaise mixture. Makes 12 servings.

My mother used to make a Cucumber-Sour Cream Salad that tasted better than anyone else's. For years, I experimented with varying amounts of sour cream, onions and cucumbers, but I could never produce just the right consistency and flavor. Then I discovered your recipe. . . it was just like Mother's. I am so delighted to have found it—and so is my family! (Nebraska) □A simple recipe for cucumbers that tastes like an elegant dish from a Swedish smorgasbord. (New York) □My husband loves cucumbers fixed in this way—he calls them those "darn good creamy cucumbers that you make"—needless to say I make them often. (Iowa)

CUCUMBER-SOUR CREAM SALAD

1 tblsp. sugar
1½ tsp. salt
1 c. dairy sour cream
3 tblsp. grated onion
2 tblsp. white vinegar or lemon juice
4½ c. thinly sliced pared cucumbers
    (6 medium)

Blend together sugar, salt, sour cream, onion and vinegar in large bowl. Add cucumbers; mix well. Cover and chill at least 2 hours. Makes 8 servings.

PICKLES
&
RELISHES

PICKLES & RELISHES

BEST-EVER BREAD-AND-BUTTERS
SWEET DILLS
WATERMELON PICKLES
EXPERT'S SWEET PICKLES
CINNAMON CUCUMBER RINGS
BLENDER KETCHUP
IOWA CORN RELISH
SLICED ZUCCHINI PICKLES
ICICLE PICKLES
HOT PEPPER RELISH
GRANDMOTHER'S SHIRLEY SAUCE
14-DAY SWEET PICKLES
CHEERFUL SWEET PICKLES
BASIC RED SAUCE
HOT DOG RELISH
CRISP-AS-ICE CUCUMBER SLICES

Please Pass the Pickles

The one quality that is most likely to put a particular pickle in the favorites category is *crisp.* "Watermelon pickles often turn out limp and soggy, but not these," many women said of FARM JOURNAL'S Watermelon Pickles, a highly popular choice. They like crisp pickles and lots of them. Every year at the end of summer, baskets are piled high with home-grown cucumbers and vegetables ready to be preserved. Everyone pitches in to help with the canning and finally rows and rows of sparkling jars are filled with tangy dills, sweet and sour vegetables, all kinds of sweet pickles and crunchy relishes.

Pickle making is an art that used to require years of experience and judgment; even Grandmother didn't always have success with her recipes. But scientific research now gives us some explanations for the puzzling failures of years back. Today's pickle makers (as these comments testify) have consistently good results using our up-to-date recipes, along with commercially made (not homemade) vinegar of a specified acid strength of 5 percent or 50 grains. And today, no careful pickle maker relies on open kettle canning—she knows that pickles, like all other canned foods, must be sterilized in a boiling water bath for safekeeping. To insure crispness in certain recipes, the sterilization time is sometimes less than 15 minutes; in such cases pickles should be packed in sterilized jars.

No matter how many batches of pickles women put up, it's never enough. Some homemakers confess to hiding jars to save them for Christmas giving! Husbands seem to be vocal about the pickles they particularly like. In fact, many men have a favorite relish that must be served with their hamburgers, eggs and baked beans.

Farm women, who have a reputation for being inventive cooks, use their home-canned pickles as ingredients, too. They add them to recipes for potato salad, egg salad, cream cheese dips and Spanish rice, for example, to give a new taste dimension to an everyday recipe. Basic Red Sauce, first printed in our Timesaving Cookbook, is a refrigerator relish specially made for use as an ingredient to flavor dips, burgers, meat loaves and vegetables.

I had never been able to duplicate my mother's pickles until I found this Bread and Butter recipe. I can eat a jar all by myself! (Idaho) ☐I'm from a large family of prize-winning home canners but everyone agrees that I make the best Bread and Butter Pickles . . . now they all use this FARM JOURNAL recipe. (Maryland) ☐My husband wants Bread and Butter Pickles on every cheeseburger he eats. Such a versatile pickle—good on sandwiches and a must when we go camping. (Wyoming)

BEST-EVER BREAD-AND-BUTTERS

40 to 50 pickling cucumbers
½ c. pickling salt
Ice cubes
1 qt. 5% acid strength vinegar
4 c. sugar
2 tblsp. mustard seeds
1 tblsp. celery seeds
1 tblsp. ground ginger
1 tsp. ground turmeric
½ tsp. white pepper
2 qts. sliced onions

Wash cucumbers; cut ⅛-inch slice off each end. Slice cucumbers, making about 4 qts. Layer cucumber slices and salt in large bowl. Cover with ice cubes. Let stand 2 to 3 hours or until cucumbers are crisp and cold. Add more ice if needed. Drain well.

Combine next seven ingredients in large kettle. Bring mixture to boiling; boil 10 minutes. Add cucumbers and onion; bring back to boiling. Immediately pack into 8 hot pint jars, filling to within ¼-inch from the top. Adjust lids.

Process in boiling water bath 15 minutes. Start to count the processing time when water in canner returns to boiling.

Remove jars. Cool on wire racks 12 to 24 hours. Check jars for airtight seal. Makes 8 pints.

My family disliked dill pickles until I made these Sweet Dills. My husband and three sons can demolish a pint of these pickles at one sitting. Every year they coax me to make more than I did last year. (Pennsylvania)   □So easy to make and economical, too. The children love them and so do I. (Missouri)   □We like these pickles because they are crisp, transparent and slightly tangy. Our grandchildren prefer them to candy when they come to visit. (Minnesota)   □This recipe for dills is outstanding. This year we grew our own dill and used fresh dill in the recipe—superb. (Kansas)   □A fantastic pickle! And so simple to make when I am extra busy in the summer. We love them tucked into a meat or fish sandwich. (Michigan)

SWEET DILLS

4 lbs. (3 to 5-inch) pickling
   cucumbers
6 c. 5% acid strength vinegar
6 c. sugar
6 tblsp. pickling salt
1½ tsp. celery seeds
1½ tsp. mustard seeds
2 large onions, thinly sliced
16 heads fresh dill

Wash cucumbers; cut ⅛-inch slice off each end. Cut cucumbers in ¼-inch crosswise slices.

Combine vinegar, sugar, salt, celery and mustard seeds in large kettle. Bring mixture to boiling.

Place 2 slices onion and 1 dill head in each of 8 hot pint jars. Pack cucumber slices into jars. Place 1 slice onion and 1 head dill on top. Pour boiling liquid over cucumbers, filling to within ¼-inch from the top. Adjust lids.

Process in boiling water bath 15 minutes. Start to count processing time as soon as jars are placed into actively boiling water.

Remove jars. Cool on wire racks 12 to 24 hours. Check jars for airtight seal. Makes 8 pints.

Never could find a recipe for Watermelon Pickles to suit me until I discovered this one . . . it's perfect and so easy to make. I actually enjoy every minute of the preparation. (Illinois) □So many watermelon pickles are limp and soggy but these are super crisp with a lovely delicate flavor. (New York) □A great favorite with the men in my family—spiced just right, they tell me. Have had many requests for the recipe. (Illinois) □Every year I make 50 jars of these watermelon pickles for the Church Bazaar—they're sold out in 20 minutes. (California)

WATERMELON PICKLES

Rind of 1 (20 lb.) watermelon
1 gal. cold water
2 tblsp. pickling salt
2 c. 5% acid strength vinegar
7 c. sugar
1 tblsp. whole cloves
2 or 3 sticks cinnamon

Choose a melon with thick, firm rind. Trim off outer green skin and pink flesh, leaving a very thin line of pink. Stamp out rind with small cookie cutter or cut into neat squares. Place in large container.

Combine 1 gal. cold water and 2 tblsp. salt; add to watermelon rind. Let stand overnight. Drain; rinse with cold water. Cover with ice water; let stand 1 hour.

Drain. Place in large kettle. Cover rind with boiling water. Bring to boiling; reduce heat and simmer until tender. Drain well.

Combine vinegar and sugar in large kettle. Tie cloves and cinnamon sticks in cheesecloth bag; add to kettle. Bring to boiling. Add rind. Cook gently until rind is clear and transparent. Remove spice bag. Turn rind and syrup into a crock and let stand 24 hours.

Drain rind; reserve syrup in large saucepan. Bring to boiling. Pack rind in 6 hot, sterilized pint jars.

Pour boiling syrup over rind, filling to within ¼-inch from the top. Adjust lids.

Process in boiling water bath 5 minutes. Start to count the processing time when water in canner returns to boiling.

Remove jars. Cool on wire racks 12 to 24 hours. Check jars for airtight seal. Makes 6 pints.

Every year I make 100 jars of your Expert's Sweet Pickles and even that isn't enough to satisfy my family—they would like them served at every meal! (New York) □Our very favorite sweet pickle because they stay crisp right down to the last jar. (Utah) □These pickles take a little time to make but they are well worth the effort—everyone raves about them! (Michigan) □Whenever I go to a church supper or group picnic I'm expected to bring a jar of my Expert's Sweets—next year I plan to make large quantities to sell for extra income. (Oregon)

EXPERT'S SWEET PICKLES

75 (3 to 3½-inch) pickling
  cucumbers (1 peck)
2 c. pickling salt
Water
10 c. sugar
5 c. 5% acid strength vinegar
18 drops oil of cinnamon
18 drops oil of cloves
2 tblsp. celery seeds

Wash cucumbers; cut ⅛-inch slice off each end. Place cucumbers in stone crock or large glass container. Combine salt and 1 gal. water in large kettle. Bring to boiling; pour over cucumbers. Cover with a heavy plate or lid that fits inside crock. Weight down with a glass jar filled with water to keep cucumbers under the brine. Cover loosely with clean cloth. Let stand at room temperature (68 to 72°) 8 days. Stir cucumbers every day to discourage the formation of a film.

On the 8th day, empty cucumbers into a large container, pouring off brine. Wash thoroughly with cold water. Cut cucumbers in half lengthwise or cut in chunks. Return to crock which has been rinsed with water.

Bring 1 gal. water in large kettle to boiling. Pour over cucumbers. Weight down and cover as before. Let stand until the 11th day.

Drain cucumbers. Return cucumbers to crock which has been rinsed with water. Combine sugar, vinegar, oils of cinnamon and cloves and celery seeds in large kettle. Bring to boiling; pour over cucumbers. Weight down and cover as before.

On the 12th day, drain syrup from cucumbers into large kettle. Bring to boiling; pour over cucumbers. Weight down and cover as before.

On the 13th day, repeat procedure of 12th day.

On the 14th day, drain syrup from cucumbers into large kettle. Pack cucumbers in hot, sterilized pint jars. Bring syrup to boiling. Pour boiling syrup over cucumbers, filling to within ¼-inch from the top. Adjust lids.

Process in boiling water bath 5 minutes. Start to count processing time as soon as jars are placed in actively boiling water.

Remove jars. Cool on wire racks 12 to 24 hours. Check jars for airtight seal. Makes 12 to 14 pints.

Every time I serve Cinnamon Cucumber Rings at a neighborhood gathering, I know I had better plan on a trip to town to make Xerox copies of this recipe . . . I have that many requests. (Nebraska)   □A great no-fuss and never-a-failure recipe for sweet pickles. Usually make six gallons a year for Christmas gifts. (Michigan)   □Every year my children ask me if I'm going to make those green pickles with the hole in the middle, as it's their very favorite one. (Illinois)   □These pickles are perfect for holiday gifts; they look and taste so special. (Iowa)

CINNAMON CUCUMBER RINGS

2 gals. large pickling cucumbers
2 c. pickling salt
8½ qts. water
1 c. 5% acid strength vinegar
1 tsp. red food color
6 c. 5% acid strength vinegar
2 c. water
12 c. sugar
4 sticks cinnamon

Wash cucumbers; cut ⅛-inch slice off each end. Cut cucumbers in thirds crosswise; remove seeds. Slice in ½-inch rings (makes about 2 gals). Place cucumber rings in stone crock or glass container. Combine salt and 8½ qts. water; pour over cucumbers. Cover with a heavy plate or lid that fits inside crock. Weight down with a glass jar filled with water to keep cucumbers under the brine. Cover loosely with clean cloth. Let stand at room temperature (68 to 72°) 5 days. Drain cucumbers.

Combine 1 c. vinegar and red food color in large kettle. Add cucumber rings and enough water to cover. Bring to boiling; reduce heat and simmer 2 hours. Drain.

Return cucumber rings to crock. Combine 6 c. vinegar, 2 c. water, sugar and cinnamon sticks in large kettle. Bring to boiling. Pour over cucumber rings. Cover and let stand overnight.

Drain cucumbers, reserving syrup in large kettle. Bring syrup to boiling and pour over cucumbers in crock. Cover and let stand overnight. Repeat this procedure 2 more times.

On the 3rd day, drain cucumbers, reserving syrup in large kettle. Pack cucumber rings in 9 hot, sterilized pint jars. Bring syrup to boiling. Pour boiling syrup over cucumbers, filling to within ¼-inch from the top. Adjust lids.

Process in boiling water bath 5 minutes. Start to count the processing time as soon as jars are placed in actively boiling water.

Remove jars. Cool on wire racks 12 to 24 hours. Check jars for airtight seal. Makes 9 pints.

Making Blender Ketchup is my favorite way of using up a lot of surplus ripe tomatoes with very little effort . . . always make several quarts at a time. (Kansas) □So easy . . . ingredients are buzzed in a blender and then put in the oven. Even on a busy day this ketchup is a cinch to make. My husband says it tastes too good to be called ketchup. (Oregon) □My grandchildren brag that I make the very best ketchup for hamburgers and French fries. This is such a quick and easy way to make ketchup, with no waste. (Pennsylvania)

BLENDER KETCHUP

48 medium tomatoes (about 8 lbs.)
2 medium sweet red peppers
2 medium green peppers
4 onions, peeled and quartered
3 c. 5% acid strength vinegar
3 c. sugar
3 tblsp. pickling salt
3 tsp. dry mustard
½ tsp. ground red pepper
½ tsp. whole allspice
1½ tsp. whole cloves
1 (3-inch) stick cinnamon

Quarter tomatoes; remove stem ends. Seed peppers and cut in strips. Put tomatoes, peppers and onion in blender container, filling jar ¾ full. Blend at high speed 4 seconds; pour into large kettle. Repeat until all vegetables are blended. Add vinegar, sugar, salt, mustard and pepper.

Tie spices in cheesecloth bag; add to kettle. Simmer in 325° oven or in electric saucepan until volume is reduced to one half. Remove spice bag. Ladle into 5 hot, sterilized pint jars, filling to within ¼-inch from the top. Adjust lids.

Process in boiling water bath 10 minutes . Start to count the processing time when water in canner returns to boiling.

Remove jars. Cool on wire rack 12 to 24 hours. Check jars for airtight seal. Makes 5 pints.

Blender Ketchup—recipe, page 106

Iowa Corn Relish—recipe, page 110

I'm a transplanted Iowa girl and love this Iowa Corn Relish. Have shared the recipe with my southern friends and neighbors—they agree it's delicious even though they had never heard of making relish from corn. (Texas) □Whenever I want to perk up a meal, I add a dish of Iowa Relish to my menu— never one kernel left! (Minnesota) □I have tried at least ten recipes for corn relish and never found one as outstanding as this. (Illinois)

IOWA CORN RELISH

20 ears sweet corn
1 c. chopped green pepper
1 c. chopped sweet red pepper
1¼ c. chopped onion
1 c. chopped celery
1½ c. sugar
1½ tblsp. mustard seeds
1 tblsp. salt
1 tsp. celery seeds
½ tsp. ground turmeric
2⅔ c. 5% acid strength vinegar
2 c. water

Cook corn in boiling water in large kettle 5 minutes. Plunge into cold water. Cut kernels from cobs making 2½ qts. Combine corn, green pepper, red pepper, onion, celery, sugar, mustard seeds, salt, celery seeds, turmeric, vinegar and water in large kettle. Bring to boiling; reduce heat and simmer 20 minutes.

Ladle mixture into 5 hot pint jars, filling to within ¼-inch from the top. Adjust lids.

Process in boiling water bath 20 minutes. Start to count the processing time when water in canner returns to boiling.

Remove jars. Cool on wire racks 12 to 24 hours. Check jars for airtight seal. Makes 5 pints.

I won my first blue ribbon with your Sliced Zucchini Pickle recipe. (Pennsylvania) □We always have a bountiful crop of zucchini. The family soon tires of it as a vegetable. I was delighted to discover this recipe. Now the family hopes the zucchini crop will be even bigger next year—that means more jars of their favorite pickle. (Indiana) □No one ever guesses that these pickles are made from zucchini. Everyone loves them. I add them to egg and tuna sandwiches for extra flavor and crunch. (New York) □A delicious addition to potato salad—makes an everyday food taste and look special. (Iowa)

SLICED ZUCCHINI PICKLES

4 qts. thinly sliced unpared zucchini
1 qt. thinly sliced onion
½ c. pickling salt
6 c. 5% acid strength cider vinegar
3 c. sugar
2 tsp. celery seeds
2 tsp. ground turmeric
1 tsp. ground mustard

Combine zucchini, onion and salt in large bowl. Cover with ice and let stand 3 hours. If needed, add more ice. Drain thoroughly.

Combine vinegar, sugar, celery seeds, turmeric and mustard in large saucepan. Bring to boiling. Add drained vegetables; return to boiling. Reduce heat and simmer 3 minutes. Immediately ladle into 6 hot, sterilized pint jars, filling to within ¼-inch from the top. Adjust lids.

Process in boiling water bath 5 minutes. Start to count the processing time when water in canner returns to boiling.

Remove jars. Cool on wire racks 12 to 24 hours. Check jars for airtight seal. Makes 6 pints.

I was searching for an excellent pickle recipe and Icicle Pickles was it. Have had more people request this recipe than any other pickle I have ever made. (Iowa)   □Have never had a failure with this recipe. I sometimes cut them into unusual shapes to serve at social occasions. (Pennsylvania)   □I always include these Icicles on any relish tray I prepare. My husband tells me I need not bother to make any other pickle. (Ohio) □Have made several Icicle Pickles in the past, but have never had such good results as with this recipe—very crisp and retain their pretty green color. (Nebraska)

ICICLE PICKLES

4 qts. (3-inch) pickling cucumbers
2 c. pickling salt
1 gal. boiling water
2½ qts. vinegar
5 lbs. sugar
2 tblsp. whole allspice

Wash cucumbers; cut ⅛-inch slice off each end. Cut cucumbers in quarters, lengthwise. Place cucumbers in stone crock or large glass container. Combine salt and boiling water; pour over cucumbers. Cover with a heavy plate or lid that fits inside crock. Weight down with a glass jar filled with water to keep cucumbers under the brine. Cover loosely with clean cloth. Let stand at room temperature (68-72°) for 7 days.

Drain cucumbers. Return cucumbers to crock which has been rinsed with water. Pour 1 gal. boiling water over cucumbers. Weight down and cover as above. Let stand 24 hours.

On the next day, repeat above procedure.

On the following day, drain cucumbers. Return cucumbers to crock which has been rinsed with water. Combine vinegar, sugar and allspice in large kettle. Heat to boiling; boil 20 minutes. Pour over cucumbers. Weight down and cover as before. Let stand 3 days.

Remove cucumbers from syrup. Pack into 5 hot, sterilized jars. Bring syrup to boiling; boil 10 minutes. Pour over pickles in jars. Adjust lids.

Process in boiling water bath 5 minutes. Start to count processing time as soon as jars are placed in actively boiling water.

Remove jars. Cool on wire racks 12 to 24 hours. Check jars for airtight seal. Makes 5 pints.

Hot Pepper Relish adds lots of zip to plain old hamburgers. When our neighbors help us out during the busy haying season, they expect Hot Pepper Relish to be included in our every meal. (Indiana) □Friends bring me their hot peppers in exchange for a share of Hot Pepper Relish. (Kansas) □This is such an easy relish to make and the end result is satisfying, colorful and delicious. My husband planted two long rows of hot pepper seeds one year and every seed sprouted. What to do with all those peppers? Hot Pepper Relish—now I make it every year. (Maryland) □This relish is starred as my favorite homemade Christmas gift for a long list of friends. (Iowa)

HOT PEPPER RELISH

18 red chili peppers
18 green chili peppers
15 medium onions
1 tblsp. salt
2½ c. vinegar
2½ c. sugar

Cut peppers in half; discard seeds. Chop peppers and onions using medium blade of food chopper. Combine chopped vegetables with salt; mix well. Cover with boiling water. Let stand 10 minutes. Drain and discard liquid. Add vinegar and sugar.

Place drained vegetables in Dutch oven. Add vinegar and sugar. Bring to a boil and simmer 20 minutes. Ladle into 6 hot, sterilized pint jars, filling to within ¼-inch from the top. Adjust lids.

Process in boiling water bath 5 minutes. Start to count the processing time when water in canner returns to boiling.

Remove jars. Cool on wire rack 12 to 24 hours. Check jars for airtight seal. Makes 6 pints.

So much cheaper and better—ten times better than store-bought chili sauce. That's the way my family feels about Grandmother's Shirley Sauce. (South Carolina)   □It's my favorite canning recipe and when mixed with horseradish, it makes a terrific shrimp cocktail sauce. (Ohio)   □This sauce has just the taste my family likes—rich full-bodied tomato flavor and it's not too heavily spiced. (Minnesota)   □ Whenever I make hamburgers, hot dogs, baked beans or French fries, the children always say, "Don't forget that yummy chili sauce". And when we empty a jar of this sauce, my husband always asks, "How much is left in the cellar?" (Kansas)

GRANDMOTHER'S SHIRLEY SAUCE

12 large tomatoes
2 large green peppers, chopped
2 large onions, chopped
2 c. sugar
2 c. 5% acid strength vinegar
2 tblsp. pickling salt

Peel and cut up tomatoes. Combine tomatoes, green peppers, onion, sugar, vinegar and salt in large kettle. Bring to boiling; reduce heat and simmer 2 hours. Immediately ladle into 3 hot, sterilized pint jars, filling to within ¼-inch from the top. Adjust lids.

Process in boiling water bath 5 minutes. Start to count processing time when water in canner returns to boiling.

Remove jars. Cool on wire racks 12 to 24 hours. Check jars for airtight seal. Makes 3 pints.

These 14-Day Sweet Pickles are extra-crisp—best tasting pickle I have ever eaten. They do take time but I never seem to get the superior flavor and texture from "quickie" recipes. (Illinois) □We're big pickle eaters—we think this pickle is very special—for salads, sandwiches and eating from the jar. (Missouri) □The directions are so explicit and easy to follow. My 17-year-old daughter learned to make pickles this year, using this recipe—she was so proud of her perfect results. (Indiana) □I have been making these pickles for 12 years and have never had a failure. I've collected many compliments, thanks to FARM JOURNAL. (Nebraska)

14-DAY SWEET PICKLES

3½ qts. (2-inch) pickling cucumbers
1 c. pickling salt
2 qts. boiling water
5 c. 5% acid strength vinegar
3 c. sugar
1½ tsp. celery seeds
4 (2-inch) sticks cinnamon
1½ c.sugar

Wash cucumbers; cut ⅛-inch slice off each end. Cut cucumbers in lengthwise halves and place in stone crock or glass container. Dissolve salt in water; pour over cucumbers. Cover with a heavy plate or lid that fits inside crock. Weight down with a glass jar filled with water to keep cucumbers under the brine. Cover loosely with clean cloth. Let stand at room temperature (68-72°) 7 days.

On the 8th day, drain cucumbers. Return to crock that has been rinsed with water. Pour 2 qts. boiling water over cucumbers. Let stand 24 hours.

Repeat above procedure two more times.

On the 11th day, drain cucumbers. Return cucumbers to crock that has been rinsed with water.

Combine vinegar, 3 c. sugar, celery seeds and cinnamon in 3-qt. saucepan. Bring to boiling; pour over cucumbers.

Repeat above procedure two more times, adding ½ c. sugar to syrup the last two times.

On the 14th day, drain cucumbers reserving liquid in 3-qt. saucepan. Pack cucumbers into 6 hot, sterilized pint jars. Add ½ c. sugar to syrup. Bring syrup to boiling. Pour boiling syrup over cucumbers, filling to within ¼-inch from the top. Adjust lids.

Process in boiling water bath 5 minutes. Start to count processing time as soon as jars are placed in actively boiling water.

Remove jars. Cool on wire racks 12 to 24 hours. Check jars for airtight seal. Makes 6 pints.

The kids call your Cheerful Sweet Pickles "Mom's Christmas Pickles" ever since I made them three years ago for the holidays. They're a family tradition now. (Pennsylvania) □Finely minced Cheerful Sweets blended into cream cheese and spread on tiny circles of bread make an attractive and tasty sandwich for showers and wedding receptions. (South Dakota) □I often vary the recipe and make several batches using green maraschino cherries instead of red. (Indiana) □They add a cheerful spot of color to our winter meals. (Iowa) □My husband always requests a small side dish of "those good pickles" to eat along with his morning eggs. (Ohio)

CHEERFUL SWEET PICKLES

9 medium ripe pickling cucumbers,
   pared
½ c. pickling salt
3½ qts. water
3½ c. sugar
2 c. 5% acid strength vinegar
1 tsp. whole cloves
2 sticks cinnamon
1 (4 oz.) jar maraschino cherries
2 tsp. red food color

Cut ⅛-inch slice off each end of pared cucumbers. Seed cucumbers and cut into cubes, making about 9 c. Place cucumbers in large bowl; sprinkle with salt. Cover with water. Let stand overnight.

Place cucumbers and liquid in large saucepan. Heat to boiling; drain well. Combine sugar and vinegar in large saucepan. Tie cloves and cinnamon in cheesecloth bag; add to saucepan. Heat to boiling. Pour over cucumbers in large bowl. Let stand overnight.

Place cucumbers and liquid in large kettle. Heat to boiling. Simmer until cucumbers are tender (do not overcook). Add undrained cherries and food color. Immediately ladle into 4 hot, sterilized pint jars, filling to within ¼-inch from the top. Adjust lids.

Process in boiling water bath 5 minutes. Start to count the processing time when water in canner returns to boiling.

Remove jars. Cool on wire racks 12 to 24 hours. Check jars for airtight seal. Makes 4 pints.

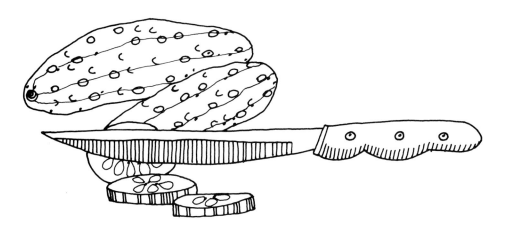

Your recipe for Basic Red Sauce is now my specialty. (Iowa) ☐I always double the recipe and keep some in the freezer. Then I just scoop out what I need for a meal. We like it as a bake-on topping for meat loaf. (California) ☐Whenever I need a dip for party snacks, I make your Basic Red Sauce. Combined with a nippy cheese, it makes a different and delicious dip. (New York) ☐I always plan to have plenty of Red Sauce on hand when the picnic barbecue season begins. It makes a great dip when mixed with cream cheese. I'm always told to bring "that good dip of yours" to card parties and club meetings. (Wisconsin)

BASIC RED SAUCE

1 c. finely chopped onion
⅓ c. cooking oil
1½ c. ketchup
½ c. water
½ c. lemon juice
¼ c. sugar
¼ c. Worcestershire sauce
2½ tsp. salt
½ tsp. pepper
4 drops Tabasco sauce

Saute onion in hot oil in 3-qt. saucepan until tender (do not brown). Add ketchup, water, lemon juice, sugar, Worcestershire sauce, salt, pepper and Tabasco sauce. Bring to a boil; reduce heat and simmer 15 minutes. Pour into storage containers. Cool slightly. Cover and store in refrigerator or freezer. Makes 2 pints.

When I serve hamburgers for lunch, a whole pint jar of Hot Dog Relish usually disappears! Best relish you've ever made, my husband tells me. (Oregon)　□A few spoonfuls of this relish makes chicken, tuna and egg salad sandwiches taste extra-special. (Ohio)　□My favorite way to use our end-of-the-season garden bounty. I'm famous for my tartar sauce. The secret—hot dog relish and sour cream stirred into the mayonnaise. (Montana)　□I never seem to make enough Hot Dog Relish to suit my family—they would like it everyday. I always hide a dozen jars for Christmas gifts. (New Jersey)

HOT DOG RELISH

3 medium carrots, pared and finely
 chopped
3 medium sweet red peppers, seeded
 and finely chopped
2 qts. finely chopped pickling
 cucumbers
2 qts. finely chopped peeled green
 tomatoes
2 qts. finely chopped onion
½ c. pickling salt
3 c. sugar
1½ c. 5% acid strength vinegar
½ tsp. cayenne pepper
2 tblsp. mixed pickling spices

Combine carrots, red peppers, cucumbers, green tomatoes and onion in large bowl. Sprinkle with salt. Let stand overnight.

Drain vegetables; place in large kettle. Add sugar, vinegar and cayenne pepper. Tie pickling spices in cheesecloth bag; add to kettle. Bring to boiling; reduce heat and simmer 45 minutes. Pour immediately into 6 hot pint jars, filling to within ¼-inch from the top. Adjust lids.

Process in boiling water bath 15 minutes. Start to count the processing time when water in canner returns to boiling.

Remove jars. Cool on wire racks 12 to 24 hours. Check jars for airtight seal. Makes 6 pints.

Crisp-as-Ice Cucumber Slices are so easy to make. This was my first attempt at making pickles and it was a huge success. The whole family loved them. Was sorry I hadn't made a triple batch . . . next year I plan to make enough to last through the winter. (Maine)   □My mother-in-law and I make many types of pickles. We both agree this is our extra-special favorite. (Indiana)   □If my family had their way these are the only pickles I would make. (Missouri)

CRISP-AS-ICE CUCUMBER SLICES

4 lbs. pickling cucumbers
8 onions, thinly sliced
2 green peppers, seeded and
   cut in strips
½ c. pickling salt
Ice cubes
4 c. sugar
4½ c. 5% acid strength vinegar
1½ tsp. ground turmeric
½ tsp. ground cloves
3½ tsp. mustard seeds

Wash cucumbers; cut ⅛-inch slice off each end. Thinly slice cucumbers, making about 4 qts. Layer cucumbers, onion, green pepper and salt in large bowl. Cover with ice cubes. Let stand 3 hours, adding more ice if needed. Drain well.

Combine sugar, vinegar, turmeric, cloves and mustard seeds in large kettle; bring to boiling. Add vegetables. Heat over low heat to scalding (do not boil). Stir mixture often to prevent scorching. Immediately ladle into 6 hot, sterilized pint jars, filling to within ¼-inch from the top. Adjust lids.

Process in boiling water bath 5 minutes. Start to count the processing time when water in canner returns to boiling.

Remove jars. Cool on wire racks 12 to 24 hours. Check jars for airtight seal. Makes 5½ pints.

YEAST
&
QUICK BREADS

YEAST & QUICK BREADS

RICH HOT ROLLS
BEST-EVER WHITE BREAD
HONEY WHOLE WHEAT BREAD
OLD-FASHIONED OATMEAL BREAD
WHOLE WHEAT BREAD
HOMEMADE WHITE BREAD
EASTER EGG BREAD
ROADSIDE POTATO BREAD
CRUSTY BROWN ROLLS
BRIOCHE
DILLY CASSEROLE BREAD
SWEDISH RYE BREAD
CRUSTY HOT BISCUITS
HONEY-FILLED COFFEE CAKE
CINNAMON LEAF RING
COOLRISE SWEET DOUGH
BANANA BREAD
CINNAMON TWIST BREAD
BUTTER CRESCENTS
SQUARE DOUGHNUTS
PUFFY POTATO DOUGHNUTS
RAISED DOUGHNUTS
COOLRISE FRENCH BREAD
ZUCCHINI NUT BREAD
REFRIGERATOR BRAN MUFFINS
SUGAR-TOP COFFEE CAKE

MMMM...Homemade Bread

Baked goods—cakes, pies, breads, cookies—had the highest number of "top favorite" nominations. And homemade bread was the winner in baked goods, edging out pie.

The wonderful smell of bread baking in the oven has traditionally drifted through country kitchens. Farm women by the thousands told us that their family won't eat "store bread." Home-baked bread is having a resurgence in urban homes, too, and commercial bakers have introduced many "old-fashioned" varieties.

Only two other recipes—Fudge Cake and Best-Ever Lemon Meringue Pie—surpassed the FARM JOURNAL Test Kitchen recipe for Rich Hot Rolls in the number of votes for top favorite! The recipe is reproduced in this collection complete with its two variations—Cinnamon Rolls and Butterscotch Rolls.

A dependable white bread recipe is a treasure, and cookbook users gave their votes to Best-Ever White Bread. The original recipe suggests doubling the ingredients and most women do, to make four plump loaves. Fewer than that don't last long in their families, they say. A whole wheat and an oatmeal bread scored second and third in loaf breads and we include the recipes. Nutrition-conscious mothers also favor homemade bread boosted with wheat germ or soy flour.

Coffee cakes and rings to serve at morning coffees were also among the popular entries. Yeast doughs, such as Honey-Filled Coffee Cake and Cinnamon Leaf Ring, are top choices when women have time to make them. Quick coffee cakes and breads are stirred up on busier days. Sugar-Top Coffee Cake, Banana Bread and Zucchini Nut Bread rated high on the list of fast-fix breads. Raised doughnuts are so popular that women voted for three recipes, one of them a puffy potato doughnut.

No bread maker's collection would be complete without company and holiday breads. Women proved this by acclaiming a good mixture of recipes, from sturdy homespun loaves to frankly fancy Easter Egg Bread and a delicate Brioche. Cherry Nut Coffee Bread and Apricot Coffee Bread, variations made from CoolRise Sweet Dough, are handsome holiday breads.

My standby for breakfast is FARM JOURNAL'S Rich Hot Rolls recipe, with all those marvelous variations. My husband tells me it's foolish to even consider trying another recipe—this is perfect. (Iowa) ☐My four daughters used this basic rich dough, spread with fillings from foreign countries, and came away with blue ribbons every time. (Montana) ☐This recipe makes an extemely light, tender dough. I use it for either cinnamon rolls or raised doughnuts. (Washington) ☐No matter how you shape them, these rolls turn out perfectly. I've made crescents, butterhorns, doughnuts and pinwheels—all are gorgeous. (Ohio) ☐I usually double the recipe and make half plain, the other half cinnamon or butterscotch. (Illinois)

RICH HOT ROLLS

¾ c. milk
½ c. shortening
½ c. sugar
1 tsp. salt
2 pkgs. active dry yeast
½ c. lukewarm water (110 to 115°)
4¼ to 4¾ c. sifted flour
2 eggs
Melted butter or regular margarine

Scald milk. Combine milk, shortening, sugar and salt in bowl. Cool to lukewarm.

Sprinkle yeast on lukewarm water; stir to dissolve.

Add 1½ c. flour to milk mixture; beat well by hand or with electric mixer at low speed 1 minute. Beat in eggs and yeast.

Gradually stir in enough remaining flour, a little at a time, to make a soft dough that leaves the sides of the bowl. Turn onto lightly floured surface; knead until smooth, satiny and no longer sticky, 8 minutes.

Place in lightly greased bowl; invert to grease top. Cover and let rise in warm place until doubled, 1 to 1½ hours. Punch down and turn onto lightly floured surface. Divide in half and shape as desired. (See How to Shape Rolls, Cinnamon Rolls and Butterscotch Rolls.)

Brush tops lightly with melted butter; let rise until doubled, 30 to 45 minutes.

Bake in 375° oven 12 to 15 minutes or until golden brown. Makes about 30 rolls.

Note: Less rich rolls can be made by reducing sugar to ¼ c. and shortening to ⅓ c. in recipe above.

How To Shape Rolls

Cloverleafs: Shape dough in long rolls 1-inch in diameter. Cut off 1-inch pieces and form each into a small ball. Place 3 balls in each greased muffin-pan cup. Balls should touch bottom of cups and fill them half full. Brush with melted butter or margarine.

Four-Leaf Clovers: Place 2-inch ball of dough in each greased muffin-pan cup. With scissors, cut surface of each ball in half and then across again to make fourths.

Butterhorns: Roll dough ¼-inch thick, brush with melted butter or margarine and cut in 12-inch circle. Cut circle in 16 pie-shaped pieces. Starting at wide or curved end, roll up. Place point end down, on greased baking sheet, 2 inches apart.

Crescents: Make like butterhorns, but curve ends of each roll on baking sheet to make crescent shapes.

Fan-Tans: Roll dough ⅛-inch thick into an oblong. Brush with melted butter or margarine. Cut in 1½-inch strips. Stack 6 strips; cut in 1½-inch pieces. Place cut side down in greased muffin-pan cups.

Pan Rolls: Shape dough in 2-inch balls. Dip in melted butter or margarine. Place in greased round layer cake pans, letting balls just touch one another.

Dinner Rolls: Shape dough in 2-inch balls. Roll each ball with floured hands until 4 inches long. Roll ends between hands to taper. Place on greased baking sheet, 2 inches apart.

Parkerhouse Rolls: Roll dough ¼-inch thick on lightly floured board; cut in rounds with 2½-inch floured biscuit or cookie cutter. Brush with melted butter. Make a crease in each round just off center with back of table knife. Fold larger side of each round over other side, overlapping slightly. Seal end edges. Brush with melted butter; place rolls about 1 inch apart on greased baking sheet.

CINNAMON ROLLS

1 recipe Rich Hot Rolls
1 c. sugar
½ c. melted butter or regular
   margarine
1 tblsp. ground cinnamon
⅔ c. raisins

Divide risen dough for Rich Hot Rolls in half. Roll each half into 16x8-inch rectangle. Combine sugar, butter and cinnamon. Spread half of mixture on each. Sprinkle each with raisins. Roll from long side as for jelly roll; seal edges. Cut in 1-inch slices. Place in 2 greased 9-inch square baking pans. Cover and let rise until doubled, about 35 minutes.

Bake in 375° oven 20 to 25 minutes or until done. Remove from pans; cool on racks. Frost with your favorite icing if you wish. Makes 32 rolls.

BUTTERSCOTCH ROLLS

½ recipe Rich Hot Rolls
¼ c. melted butter or regular
   margarine
⅓ c. brown sugar, firmly packed
1 tsp. ground cinnamon
¼ c. melted butter or regular
   margarine
½ c. brown sugar, firmly packed
1 tblsp. light corn syrup
⅓ c. finely chopped pecans

Roll half of risen dough into 16x8-inch rectangle. Brush with ¼ c. butter. Sprinkle with combined ⅓ c. brown sugar and cinnamon. Roll from long side as for jelly roll; seal edges. Cut in 1-inch slices.

Pour ¼ c. butter into 9-inch square baking pan. Grease sides of pan. Stir ½ c. brown sugar and corn syrup into butter; mix well. Heat slowly, stirring constantly, until mixture is syrupy and spreads evenly over bottom of pan. Remove from heat. Sprinkle with pecans. Place rolls over syrup mixture. Cover and let rise until doubled, 30 to 45 minutes.

Bake in 375° oven 20 minutes or until done. Cool 3 minutes in pan or rack. Invert pan on rack and remove pan. Makes 16 rolls.

Six blue ribbons and two Wheat Growers' awards for best loaf of white bread—that's what your recipe for Best-Ever White Bread has won for me. (Washington) □My grandson and I have an understanding. When his baseball team wins, I bake him a loaf of this bread—he says it is the best-ever! (Indiana) □My son never eats the crust of bread, but he does when I make this recipe. My father makes a special trip over when he knows I'm going to bake this bread. My husband's friends linger around the door when the bread is baking. They eat half a loaf hot from the oven—just plain—no butter, no jelly. Doesn't need it they tell me. (Michigan)

BEST-EVER WHITE BREAD

2 c. milk
2 tblsp. sugar
2 tsp. salt
1 tblsp. shortening
1 pkg. active dry yeast
¼ c. lukewarm water (110 to 115°)
6 to 6½ c. sifted flour

Scald milk in saucepan. Stir in sugar, salt and shortening in large bowl. Cool to lukewarm.

Sprinkle yeast on lukewarm water; stir to dissolve. Add yeast and 3 c. flour to milk mixture. Beat with electric mixer at medium speed until smooth, about 2 minutes, scraping bowl occasionally.

Add enough remaining flour, a little at a time, first by spoon and then with hands to make a dough that leaves the sides of the bowl. Turn onto lightly floured board; cover and let rest 10 minutes.

Knead until smooth and elastic, 8 to 10 minutes. Round up into a ball and put into lightly greased bowl; turn dough over to grease top. Cover and let rise in warm place until doubled, about 1¼ hours. Punch down, cover and let rise again until almost doubled, about 45 minutes.

Turn onto board and shape into ball. Divide in half. Shape into loaves and place in 2 greased 9x5x3-inch loaf pans. Cover and let rise until doubled, about 1 hour.

Bake in 400° oven 35 minutes or until golden brown and bread tests done. Remove from pans; cool on racks. Makes 2 loaves.

My kitchen smells wonderful when I bake Honey Whole Wheat Bread. I make this bread at least once a week and my family thinks I am the greatest bread baker in the county. (West Virginia)   □This bread is full of country flavor and fragrance. It's absolutely fool-proof and easy to make with good directions. (North Dakota)   □We like the good wholesome quality and wonderful taste. And it's high-fiber and high-protein, too. (California)   □This bread has so much more substance and flavor than other whole wheats. Delicious served hot or cold, plain or toasted. (Iowa)   □If you think this bread is good warm from the oven, you should try it toasted—tastes even better. (Kansas)   □There were many more entries this year of whole wheat and natural grain breads at our county fair—your Honey Whole Wheat still won the blue ribbon for me. (Oregon)

HONEY WHOLE WHEAT BREAD

2 pkgs. active dry yeast
½ c. lukewarm water (110 to 115°)
6 tblsp. shortening
¼ c. honey
4½ c. lukewarm water
   (110 to 115°)
4 c. whole wheat flour
½ c. instant mashed potatoes
   (not reconstituted)
½ c. nonfat dry milk
1 tblsp. salt
6½ to 8 c. sifted flour

Sprinkle yeast on ½ c. lukewarm water; stir to dissolve.

Melt shortening in 6-qt. saucepan; remove from heat. Add honey and 4½ c. lukewarm water.

Mix whole wheat flour (stirred before measuring), instant potatoes, dry milk and salt. Add to saucepan; beat until smooth.

Add yeast and beat to blend. Then with wooden spoon mix in enough flour, a little at a time, to make a dough that leaves the sides of the pan. Turn onto lightly floured surface and knead until smooth and satiny and small bubbles appear, 8 to 10 minutes.

Place in lightly greased bowl; turn dough over to grease top. Cover and let rise in warm place until doubled, 1 to 1½ hours. Punch down dough, turn onto board and divide in thirds. Cover and let rest 5 minutes. Shape into 3 loaves and place in greased 9x5x3-inch loaf pans. Cover and let rise until doubled, about 1 hour.

Bake in 400° oven about 50 minutes or until bread tests done. Remove from pans and cool on wire racks. Makes 3 loaves.

Note: You may use 1 c. mashed potatoes in place of instant potatoes. Combine with the honey-water mixture.

I chose to make this Old-Fashioned Oatmeal Bread because the ingredients sounded so good. I wasn't disappointed, it's a delicious bread. (Ohio)   □Never make less than four loaves of this bread at a time (double recipe). My family loves it, especially toasted. I cut it extra thick and grill on both sides. (Nebraska)   □I have made many friends happy with a gift loaf of this oatmeal bread. It's the most delicious oatmeal bread I have ever made—fantastic seller at bake sales. (Michigan)   □I make two batches of this oatmeal bread every week—never can seem to make enough to satisfy my family. They often decide to have another slice of bread and skip dessert. (Missouri)

OLD-FASHIONED OATMEAL BREAD

2 c. milk
2 c. quick rolled oats
¼ c. brown sugar, firmly packed
1 tblsp. salt
2 tblsp. shortening
1 pkg. active dry yeast
½ c. lukewarm water (110 to 115°)
5 c. sifted flour
1 egg white
1 tblsp. water
Rolled oats

Scald milk in saucepan. Stir into 2 c. rolled oats, brown sugar, salt and shortening in large bowl. Cool to lukewarm.

Sprinkle yeast on lukewarm water; stir to dissolve.

Add yeast and 2 c. flour to milk mixture. Beat with electric mixer at medium speed 2 minutes, scraping the bowl occasionally. Or beat with spoon until batter is smooth.

Add enough remaining flour, a little at a time, to make a soft dough that leaves the sides of the bowl. Turn onto floured surface. Knead until dough is smooth and elastic, 8 to 10 minutes. Place in lightly greased bowl; turn dough over to grease top. Cover and let rise in warm place until doubled, 1 to 1¼ hours. Punch down and let rise again until nearly doubled, about 30 minutes.

Turn onto board and divide in half. Round up to make 2 balls. Cover and let rest 10 minutes. Shape into two loaves and place in 2 greased 9x5x3-inch loaf pans. Let rise until almost doubled, about 1 hour and 15 minutes. Beat together egg white and 1 tblsp. water. Brush tops of loaves with egg white mixture. Sprinkle with rolled oats.

Bake in 375° oven 40 minutes or until bread tests done. (If bread starts to brown too much, cover loosely with sheet of aluminum foil after baking 15 minutes.) Remove from pans; cool on racks. Makes 2 loaves.

This Whole Wheat Bread disappears fast at our house. I bake it twice a week—miniature loaves for the youngsters' lunchboxes and big loaves for my husband's lunch sandwiches. He likes it sliced lengthwise and spread generously with butter. He heats it himself in the microwave oven for a midmorning snack when he's at home. The hired men love it, too. (Texas) □Best whole wheat bread I have ever made. I bake it in one-pound coffee cans—makes a pretty loaf and generous sandwiches. (Nebraska) □My family enjoys the delicious nutty flavor and now they all prefer it to white bread. I enjoy making it because of the simplicity and the outstanding results—and it's economical, too. (Pennsylvania)

WHOLE WHEAT BREAD

1 pkg. active dry yeast
¼ c. lukewarm water (110 to 115°)
½ c. brown sugar, firmly packed
1 tblsp. salt
2½ c. lukewarm water (110 to 115°)
¼ c. shortening
3½ c. whole wheat flour
4 c. sifted flour

Sprinkle yeast on ¼ c. lukewarm water; stir to dissolve. Dissolve brown sugar and salt in 2½ c. lukewarm water in large bowl. Add shortening, whole wheat flour, 1 c. flour and yeast. Beat thoroughly to mix well.

Stir in enough remaining flour to make a dough that leaves the sides of the bowl. Turn out on floured surface. Cover and let rest for 10 minutes. Knead until smooth and elastic, about 10 minutes.

Place in greased bowl; turn dough over to grease top. Cover and let rise in warm place until doubled, about 1½ hours.

Punch down. Turn onto floured surface and divide in half; round up each half to make a ball. Cover and let rest 10 minutes.

Shape into loaves and place in 2 greased 9x5x3-inch loaf pans. Let rise until dough reaches top of pan on sides and the top of loaf is well rounded above pan, about 1¼ hours.

Bake in 375° oven 45 minutes or until bread tests done. Cover loosely with sheet of aluminum foil the last 20 minutes, if necessary, to prevent excessive browning. Remove from pans; cool on racks. Makes 2 loaves.

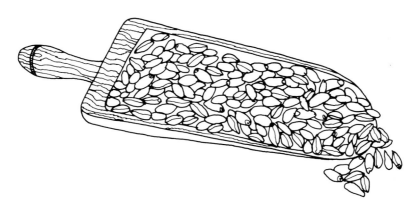

My mother and I have been making your recipe for Homemade White Bread for ten years. It's the best basic white bread recipe we have ever found and it makes four large plump loaves. (Massachusetts)   □My husband and I farm 1200 acres, so there isn't much spare time to bake bread. But when I do, it's always this recipe. Even our four-year-old son helps to knead. We like it for dessert, spread with soft butter and homemade grape jelly. (Indiana)   □I made this bread for a church banquet. Now my bread is requested for every banquet—both white and the whole wheat variation. (Ohio)   □I slice the bread 1½-inches thick and dip in egg and milk. Makes the best French toast I've ever tasted. (Kansas)

HOMEMADE WHITE BREAD

3 pkgs. active dry yeast
½ c. lukewarm water (110 to 115°)
½ c. sugar
4 tsp. salt
⅓ c. melted shortening
5 c. water
16 to 18 c. sifted flour

Sprinkle yeast on lukewarm water; stir to dissolve.

Combine sugar, salt, shortening and water in 5-qt. bowl. Stir in 8 c. flour. Add yeast and enough of remaining flour (8 to 10 c.) to make a stiff dough that leaves the sides of the bowl.

Knead on lightly floured surface until smooth and satiny, about 8 minutes. Place in greased bowl; turn to bring greased side up. Cover; let rise in warm place until doubled, about 1½ hours. Punch down dough. Turn out on floured surface.

Divide in half. Set aside one half to rise again. Divide other portion in half; shape each half into smooth ball; let rest 10 minutes. Shape into loaves; place in 2 greased 9x5x3-inch loaf pans. Grease top slightly; cover and let rise until doubled, about 1 hour. Bake in 400° oven 40 to 50 minutes. Immediately turn out of pans on rack. Cool thoroughly.

When portion of dough set for second rising is doubled, punch down and repeat shaping, rising and baking process.

Wrap or package loaves individually as soon as they cool. Seal, label, date and freeze.

Recommended storage time: 3 months to a year.

To serve, let thaw in wrapper at room temperature (on rack to allow air circulation) and heat in foil wrapper in 375° oven 20 minutes. Foil may be opened for last 5 minutes to crisp the crust. Makes 4 loaves.

Whole Wheat Bread: Substitute whole wheat flour for half the white flour.

Raisin Coffee Bread: Make 3 loaves and knead ½ c. raisins into fourth loaf just before shaping. Place in greased 8-inch square pan to rise. Before baking, brush top with melted butter and sprinkle with cinnamon and sugar.

Potato Bread: Reduce amount of water to 3 c. Add 2 c. instant mashed potatoes to water mixture before adding flour and yeast.

Milk Bread: Substitute 5 c. scalded milk for 5 c. water. Add sugar, salt and shortening. Cool to lukewarm before adding yeast.

Easter Egg Bread—recipe, page 142

Sugar-Top Coffee Cake—recipe, page 180

Easter Egg Bread has been a tradition in our family for years. Sunday morning breakfast on Easter would be dismal without this handsome coffee ring. My married daughter moved to Australia and took the recipe with her. Many of her neighbors are baking this every Easter—an international recipe. (Washington) □We always had this bread for breakfast on Easter Sunday when I was growing up. No one knew what happened to the recipe. Then I found it in your cookbook. Even though it was the middle of July, I rushed into the kitchen and made it. (New York) □On Easter Morning our children invite their friends in to sample the special bread their Mom has made. (Pennsylvania)

EASTER EGG BREAD

12 eggs in shell, uncooked
Easter egg coloring
½ c. milk
½ c. sugar
1 tsp. salt
½ c. shortening
Grated rind of 2 lemons
2 pkgs. active dry yeast
½ c. lukewarm water (110 to 115°)
2 eggs
4½ c. sifted flour
1 egg, beaten
Tiny colored candies

Wash 12 uncooked eggs. Tint shells with egg coloring; set aside.

Scald milk; pour over sugar, salt, shortening and lemon rind in bowl. Cool to lukewarm.

Sprinkle yeast on lukewarm water; stir to dissolve. Add to milk mixture with the 2 eggs and 2½ c. flour. Beat until smooth.

Stir in enough remaining flour, a little at a time, to form a dough that is easy to handle. Turn onto lightly floured board and knead until smooth and elastic, 5 to 8 minutes. Place in lightly greased bowl; turn dough over to grease top. Cover and let rise in warm place until doubled, about 1 hour.

Punch down; cover and let rise again until almost doubled, about 30 minutes.

Shape dough into 2 large braided rings or 12 individual rings (directions follow).

Cover; let rise until doubled.

Brush evenly with 1 beaten egg. Sprinkle with tiny decorating candies.

Bake in 375° oven 15 minutes for individual rings, 20 minutes for large rings or until lightly browned. Serve warm. Makes 2 large or 12 individual rings.

Note: Easter Egg Bread can be baked the day before. Refrigerate. At serving time, reheat in 350° oven 8 minutes.

Large Rings: Divide dough into 4 parts. Form each part into a 36-inch rope. On a greased baking sheet, shape 2 of the ropes into a very loosely braided ring, leaving space for 6 eggs. Repeat with other 2 ropes of dough for a second ring. Insert 6 tinted eggs in spaces in each ring.

Individual Rings: Divide dough into 12 parts. Form each part into a ring around a tinted egg.

Roadside Potato Bread—just plain good eating with home-churned butter. (New York)   □Potatoes seem to give a better-flavored and textured bread. I've used both prepared and instant potatoes with excellent results. I invented my own variations using herbs and cheese. I've even made butterscotch rolls from the basic dough. (Idaho)   □This bread stays fresh and moist longer than most homemade breads. It's great toasted. Sometimes I add wheat germ for a slightly nutty flavor. (Nebraska)   □My family of seven declares that this is the best bread they have ever eaten—even better than Grandmother's and she's an outstanding bread maker. (California)

ROADSIDE POTATO BREAD

3½ c. milk
6 tblsp. sugar
6 tblsp. butter
2 tsp. salt
¼ c. instant mashed potatoes (not reconstituted)
2 pkgs. active dry yeast
½ c. lukewarm water (110 to 115°)
10 to 11 c. sifted flour
3 tblsp. cornmeal

Scald milk in saucepan. Stir into sugar, butter, salt and instant mashed potatoes in large bowl. Cool to lukewarm.

Sprinkle yeast on lukewarm water; stir to dissolve. Add yeast and 4 c. flour to milk mixture. Beat 2 minutes with electric mixer at medium speed, scraping bowl occasionally. Or beat by hand until smooth.

Add enough remaining flour, a little at a time, to make a dough that leaves the sides of bowl.

Turn onto lightly floured surface. Cover and let rest 10 to 15 minutes. Knead until smooth, about 10 minutes. Place in greased bowl; turn dough over to grease top. Cover and let rise in warm place until doubled, 1½ to 2 hours. Punch down dough; cover and let rise again until doubled, about 45 minutes.

Turn onto floured surface and divide in 3 equal parts; round up in balls. Cover; let rest 10 minutes.

Meanwhile, grease three 8½x4½x2½-inch loaf pans. Sprinkle bottoms and sides of pans with corn-meal (1 tblsp. to each pan).

Shape dough into loaves. Place in pans; cover and let rise until doubled, 50 to 60 minutes.

Bake in 375° oven 45 minutes or until loaves are rich brown and have a hollow sound when tapped with fingers. Remove from pans; cool on racks. Makes 3 loaves.

I taught my friend to make these Crusty Brown Rolls and she won a blue ribbon her first time at the fair. (Montana) □This is the first recipe for dinner rolls that I have ever been able to make successfully every time. (Nebraska) □My mother-in-law who is a gourmet cook gave me high praise on these rolls. They taste like rolls that I have been served in European countries but I could never duplicate the recipe. (Kansas) □We like the crispy crust on these rolls—I always plan to make enough to freeze some for later. So good with homemade vegetable soup for lunch on a winter day. (Michigan)

CRUSTY BROWN ROLLS

2 pkgs. active dry yeast
1¾ c. lukewarm water (110 to 115°)
4 tsp. sugar
2 tsp. salt
2 tblsp. melted shortening
6½ to 7 c. sifted flour
3 egg whites, beaten stiff
1 egg white
1 tblsp. water

Sprinkle yeast on lukewarm water in mixing bowl; stir to dissolve. Add sugar, salt, shortening and 2 c. flour; beat well. Add egg whites. Stir in enough remaining flour to make a soft dough that leaves the sides of bowl.

Turn out on lightly floured surface. Knead dough until smooth and elastic and tiny blisters show on the surface (about 5 minutes).

Place in a lightly greased bowl; turn dough over to grease top. Cover with a damp cloth.

Let rise in a warm place until doubled, about 1 hour. Punch down.

You may shape the dough at this point. For superior results, let the dough rise again until doubled; then punch it down and shape.

Follow directions for shaping given with each type roll (see Variations).

Place rolls on greased baking sheets sprinkled lightly with cornmeal. Beat slightly 1 egg white with 1 tblsp. water. Brush on rolls as directed for each variation.

Bake in 425° oven 20 minutes or until brown and crusty. Place a large shallow pan of boiling water on the bottom of oven to provide steam while the rolls bake. This makes the rolls crusty. Makes about 3 dozen rolls.

French Rolls: Shape raised dough in 3-inch balls. Flatten to make 4-inch circles or 6-inch tapered oblongs ¾-inch thick. Use a very sharp knife or razor to make shallow cuts about ¼-inch deep on top. Place on baking sheet; brush with egg mixture. Sprinkle with poppy or sesame seeds. Let rise until doubled; brush again with egg mixture and bake.

Onion Rolls: Shape raised dough in 3-inch round rolls ½-inch thick; make hollow in centers with fingers. Fill with an onion mixture made by soaking 3 tblsp. instant minced onions in 3 tblsp. cold water, then drained and mixed with 1 tblsp. poppy seeds. Brush with egg mixture. Let rise until doubled; brush again with egg mixture and bake.

Salty Caraway Crescents: Divide the raised dough into 4 portions. Roll each portion into a very thin 16-inch square. Cut each into 16 (4-inch) squares. Roll each, starting at a corner, diagonally to opposite corner; seal, curve ends and roll gently under the palms of the hands to lengthen slightly. Place on baking sheet. Brush with egg mixture. Let rise until doubled; brush again with egg mixture. Sprinkle with coarse salt and caraway seeds and bake.

Italian Bread Sticks: Divide raised dough into 4 portions; roll each to 7x4-inch rectangle. Cut in 8 (½-inch) strips. Roll strips to make 8-inches long. Place on baking sheet; brush with water. Let rise until doubled; brush with water and bake.

Crusty Brown Rolls—recipe, page 146

148

Brioche—recipe, page 149

I always thought Brioche would be difficult to make—this recipe is so easy and elegant. (Vermont) □Such a light, delicate, golden roll. They're considered a top treat at our house—so good. (Kansas) □A recipe that's won many prizes for me. These rolls have such a fine texture and delicate lemon flavor—friends and family think I'm a fantastic cook. (West Virginia) □Whenever I serve these rolls at a Sunday morning coffee after church, everyone's impressed. I sit back, collect the compliments and give credit to FARM JOURNAL—I feel like such an accomplished cook. (Maryland) □Our favorite roll for family gatherings. They are so different from ordinary rolls. The little knob on top looks so pretty. (Oregon)

BRIOCHE

1 c. milk
½ c. butter or regular margarine
1 tsp. salt
½ c. sugar
2 pkgs. active dry yeast
¼ c. lukewarm water (110 to 115°)
4 eggs, beaten
1 tsp. grated lemon rind
5 c. sifted flour
Melted butter or regular margarine

Scald milk. Pour over ½ c. butter, salt and sugar in bowl. Cool to lukewarm.

Sprinkle yeast on lukewarm water; stir to dissolve.

Add eggs, lemon rind and yeast to milk mixture. Beat in flour, a little at a time, to make a soft dough you can handle.

Turn onto floured surface, knead lightly until dough is smooth and satiny. Place in greased bowl; turn dough over to grease top. Cover and let rise in warm place until doubled, about 2 hours. Punch down and turn out on floured surface. Knead lightly.

Shape two thirds of dough into smooth balls about 2 inches in diameter. Shape remaining dough in 1-inch balls. Place large balls in greased muffin-pan cups. Flatten balls slightly; make a deep indentation in each with finger or the handle of a wooden spoon. Shape small balls like teardrops and set one firmly in the indentation in each ball. Brush with melted butter. Cover and let rise in warm place until doubled, about 1 hour.

Bake in 425° oven about 10 minutes. Remove from pans at once. Place on racks. Serve warm; or wrap cold rolls in aluminum foil and heat a few minutes in oven before serving. Makes 3 dozen rolls.

Dilly Casserole Bread—delicious and easy-to-make. A great way to use cottage cheese. I sprinkle the warm baked loaf with coarse salt—looks pretty and tastes good. (Kansas)   □A bread that's especially good with beef roasts, steaks and barbecues. (Arizona)   □A favorite summer meal with our family—crusty fried chicken and Dilly Casserole Bread along with a crunchy tossed salad. The bread has a good texture and flavor—makes great sandwiches for a picnic. Really couldn't do without this recipe, it fits into so many of my menu plans. (Colorado)

DILLY CASSEROLE BREAD

1 pkg. active dry yeast
¼ c. lukewarm water (110 to 115°)
1 c. large curd creamed cottage
  cheese
2 tblsp. sugar
1 tblsp. instant minced onion
1 tblsp. butter or regular margarine
2 tsp. dill seeds
1 tsp. salt
¼ tsp. baking soda
1 egg
2¼ to 2½ c. sifted flour

Sprinkle yeast on lukewarm water; stir to dissolve.

Heat cottage cheese in saucepan until lukewarm. Combine cottage cheese, sugar, onion, butter, dill seeds, salt, baking soda, egg and yeast in bowl.

Add flour, a little at a time, to make a stiff batter; beat well after each addition. Cover and let rise in warm place until doubled, 30 to 40 minutes.

Bake in 350° oven 40 to 50 minutes. Cover with aluminum foil last 15 minutes of baking if necessary to prevent excessive browning. Remove from casserole; cool on rack. Makes 1 loaf.

When my son comes home from college, he heads for the kitchen. He knows I have baked a loaf of Swedish Rye Bread just for him. (Wisconsin)   □Can't beat this bread for nutritive value, excellent taste and handsome appearance. (New York) □It's an easy bread to make, but more importantly it has a true rye flavor. Never lasts long when I make it. (Iowa)   □Our Extension class had a foreign dish dinner. I volunteered to bring the Swedish Rye Bread. Now I am asked to bring this bread to every foreign dinner we have. The recipe has been written out at least 50 times. (Missouri)   □A moist, tender bread with just the right amount of rye flavor.

SWEDISH RYE BREAD SUPREME

¼ c. brown sugar, firmly packed
¼ c. light molasses
1 tblsp. salt
2 tblsp. shortening
1½ c. boiling water
1 pkg. active dry yeast
¼ c. lukewarm water (110 to 115°)
2½ c. rye flour
2 to 3 tblsp. caraway seeds
3½ to 4 c. sifted flour
Melted butter or regular margarine

Combine brown sugar, molasses, salt and shortening in large bowl. Add boiling water and stir until sugar is dissolved. Cool to lukewarm.

Sprinkle yeast on lukewarm water; stir to dissolve.

Stir rye flour into brown sugar-molasses mixture, beating well. Stir in yeast and caraway seeds; beat by hand until smooth.

Add enough flour, a little at a time, to make a smooth soft dough. Turn onto lightly floured surface. Knead until satiny and elastic, about 10 minutes. Place dough in lightly greased bowl; turn dough over to grease top. Cover and let rise in warm place until dough is doubled, 1½ to 2 hours.

Punch down dough; turn dough onto lightly floured surface and divide in half. Round up dough to make 2 balls. Cover and let rest 10 minutes. Shape into loaves and place in 2 greased 8½x4½x2½-inch loaf pans. Cover and let rise in a warm place until almost doubled, 1½ to 2 hours.

Bake in 375° oven 25 to 30 minutes or until bread tests done. Cover with aluminum foil the last 15 minutes if loaves are browning too fast. Remove from pans; cool on racks. Brush loaves with melted butter while warm for a soft crust. Makes 2 loaves.

Orange-Flavored Rye Bread: Omit caraway seeds and use instead 2 tblsp. grated orange peel.

Anise-Flavored Rye Bread: Omit caraway seeds and use instead 1 tsp. anise seeds.

Round Loaf Rye Bread: Shape the 2 balls of dough by flattening them slightly instead of shaping into oblongs. Place loaves on greased baking sheet. Let rise and bake as directed above.

Crusty Hot Biscuits rise higher and are lighter than any other biscuit I have ever made. (Illinois) □My family devours these biscuits, either with soft butter and honey or topped with chicken and gravy. (New York) □Since I made these great biscuits, my family won't eat purchased refrigerator biscuits. These are tops—so tender and flaky and easy to make. (Wyoming) □I'm always looking for a recipe that's a bit different. The egg and lard in these biscuits makes them unusual. I've served them to company many times and it's my husband's most requested hot bread. (Colorado)

CRUSTY HOT BISCUITS

2¼ c. sifted flour
4 tsp. baking powder
½ tsp. cream of tartar
½ tsp. salt
2 tblsp. sugar
⅓ c. lard
⅔ c. milk
1 egg

Sift together flour, baking powder, cream of tartar, salt and sugar into bowl. Cut in lard to make coarse crumbs. Add milk, then the egg. Mix with fork until dough follows fork around bowl.

Knead on floured surface five or six times. Roll or pat to ½-inch thickness; cut with 2-inch cutter. Place on ungreased baking sheet.

Bake in 450° oven 10 to 12 minutes or until golden brown. Remove from baking sheet. Serve warm. Makes 16 medium biscuits.

Crusty Hot Biscuits—recipe, page 154

Honey-Filled Coffee Cake—recipe, page 156

Cinnamon Leaf Ring—recipe, page 158

Our daughter won a 4-H trophy with your recipe for Honey-Filled Coffee Cake. (Illinois)   □It has now become our favorite homemade gift. (Wyoming)   □This recipe reminds me of my childhood. My mother made a recipe similar to this but not half as good—I'm so glad I found this recipe. (Minnesota)   □An excellent coffee cake—dependable, flavorful and beautiful—rates an A-plus on my recipe cards. (Massachusetts)   □My husband is fond of any recipe that uses honey—but this coffee cake is the very best, he tells me. A recipe that's reminiscent of my Hungarian mother's coffee cake—only this does taste and look more special than hers did. (Michigan)

HONEY-FILLED COFFEE CAKE

2 pkgs. active dry yeast
¼ c. lukewarm water (110 to 115°)
1 c. milk
½ c. shortening
2 tsp. salt
¼ c. sugar
2 eggs, beaten
4½ c. sifted flour
Honey Filling (recipe follows)
Honey Glaze (recipe follows)
Melted butter or regular margarine

Sprinkle yeast over lukewarm water; stir to dissolve. Scald milk in saucepan. Stir into shortening, salt and sugar in large bowl. Cool until lukewarm.

Add eggs, yeast and 1 c. flour. Beat 2 minutes with electric mixer at medium speed; scrape bowl occasionally. Gradually add enough flour to make a soft dough that leaves the sides of the bowl. Turn onto floured surface. Knead until smooth.

Place dough in greased bowl; turn dough over to grease top. Cover and let rise in warm place until doubled, about 1½ hours.

Punch down dough and let rest 10 minutes. Turn out on floured surface. Divide dough in half. Roll out half of dough to 16x12-inch rectangle. Brush with melted butter and spread with half of Honey Filling.

Roll up like jelly roll; seal edges. Cut in 1-inch slices. Place slices in greased 10-inch tube pan so they barely touch. Arrange remaining slices in layers, covering up the spaces—with no slice directly on top of the other. Prepare remaining dough in same manner. Cover and let rise in warm place until doubled, about 30 minutes.

Bake in 350° oven 45 to 60 minutes or until sides and top are well browned. (If bread browns too soon, cover with aluminum foil the last half of the baking time.) Loosen coffee cake from pan; cool on rack. Immediately pour Honey Glaze over coffee cake. Makes 1 coffee cake.

HONEY FILLING

½ c. honey
¼ c. sugar
1 tsp. grated orange rind
1 tblsp. orange juice
1 tsp. ground cinnamon
⅓ c. chopped raisins
⅓ c. finely chopped walnuts
1 tblsp. melted butter or regular
   margarine

Combine all ingredients in bowl; mix well.

HONEY GLAZE

½ c. honey
½ c. sugar
1 tblsp. butter or regular margarine
1 tblsp. grated orange rind

Combine honey, sugar, butter and orange rind in saucepan. Bring to a boil. Reduce heat and simmer 5 minutes or until thick.

We love the cinnamony-sugar taste of Cinnamon Leaf Ring. It bakes up into a very elegant crown shape with its own sugar glaze. (Texas) □Such a light coffee cake. The recipe is easy to follow, it looks terrific and tastes delicious. (New York) □I divide the dough in half and make a coffee ring and then a batch of sweet rolls—a great family favorite. (Iowa) □I bake the dough in small angel cake pans and give as gifts to friends—always a hit. (Illinois) □Everyone exclaims over this coffee ring whenever I serve it at a coffee. I sometimes twist into a braid. (Washington) □Our Sunday mornings are rush-rush-rush. I make Cinnamon Leaf Ring on Saturday and reheat it for Sunday breakfast. (Indiana)

CINNAMON LEAF RING

2 c. milk, scalded
2 pkgs. active dry yeast
¾ c. shortening
¼ c. butter or regular margarine
½ c. sugar
2 tsp. salt
4 egg yolks or 2 eggs, beaten
6 c. sifted flour
1 c. melted butter or regular margarine
2 tblsp. ground cinnamon
2 c. sugar

Cool milk to lukewarm (110°); sprinkle yeast over top. Let stand to soften.

Cream shortening and ¼ butter; add ½ c. sugar and salt. Cream together until light and fluffy. Add egg yolks, yeast mixture and enough flour to make soft dough. Knead until smooth and elastic on lightly floured cloth or board. Place in greased bowl; cover and let rise until doubled (about 1 hour).

Divide dough in half. Roll out dough to ¼-inch thickness. Cut into rounds with 2-inch biscuit cutter. Dip each round in melted butter and then in combined 2 tblsp. cinnamon and 2 c. sugar. Place rounds on end in two well-buttered 8½-inch ring molds. Let rise until doubled, about 30 minutes.

Bake in 350° oven 25 minutes or until done. Cool in pans on racks a few minutes. Turn out on racks. Makes 2 coffee cakes.

Kolaches: Use ½ recipe basic dough. Shape into small balls (about 1½ inches) and place on greased baking sheets; let rise. Brush with melted butter or margarine. Make deep hole in center of each with thumb; then press out with forefinger to make hole larger. Fill them with Apricot or Prune Filling (recipe follows). Bake in 375° oven about 15 minutes. Makes 4 dozen.

Apricot or Prune Filling: Cook together slowly, stirring until thickened: 2 c. dried apricots, cut fine (or 2 c. mashed cooked prunes), ¾ c. sugar, ¾ c. water and 1 tblsp. lemon juice. Cool.

Orange Twists: Use ½ recipe basic dough. Add 1½ tsp. grated orange rind to dough. Divide in half. Roll into 18x10-inch rectangles. Spread with well-blended mixture of grated rind of 1 orange, ¾ c. sugar and ⅓ c. soft butter or margarine. Roll up lengthwise; cut into 1½-inch slices. With back of shears, indent center of each slice. Place on greased baking sheet and let rise. Bake in 400° oven 15 to 20 minutes. While still warm, brush with following glaze: Bring to boil ½ c. sugar, ¼ c. white corn syrup and ¼ c. hot water; simmer 1 minute, stirring once or twice. Set aside to cool until rolls are removed from oven. Makes about 4 dozen rolls.

Whenever I bake CoolRise Sweet Dough, my grandchildren say that Grandma's house smells so good. They love the homemade treat. I want them to remember our home with love. (California) □A handy, no-fuss dough—allows a busy farm wife to squeeze homemade rolls into a hectic schedule. (Iowa) □I make this dough into cinnamon rolls at least once a week. Call this my "good neighbor bread" as I take these rolls to friends when they are ill—a welcome treat. (Wisconsin) □At Christmastime, I roll out the dough, spread with canned cherry pie filling, and shape into candy canes—a homemade treat for drop-in guests. (Illinois)

COOLRISE SWEET DOUGH

5 to 6 c. sifted flour
2 pkgs. active dry yeast
½ c. sugar
1½ tsp. salt
½ c. softened butter or regular
  margarine
1½ c. hot water (120 to 130°)
2 eggs

Combine 2 c. flour, undissolved yeast, sugar and salt in large bowl. Stir well to blend. Add softened butter. Add hot water to bowl all at once.

Beat with electric mixer at medium speed 2 minutes, scraping bowl occasionally.

Add eggs and 1 c. more flour. Beat with electric mixer at high speed 1 minute or until thick and elastic, scraping bowl occasionally.

Gradually stir in just enough remaining flour with wooden spoon to make a soft dough that leaves the sides of bowl. Turn onto floured surface. Round up into ball. Knead 5 to 10 minutes or until dough is smooth and elastic. Cover with plastic wrap, then a towel. Let rest 20 minutes. Punch down.

Divide and shape as desired (see Cherry Nut Coffee Bread, Apricot Coffee Cake, CoolRise Twirls and Mexican Sweet Rolls).

Refrigerate 2 to 24 hours at moderately cold setting. When ready to bake, remove from refrigerator. Uncover. Let stand 10 minutes. Puncture any surface bubbles with oiled toothpick just before baking.

Bake in 375° oven 20 to 25 minutes or until done. (Bake on lower oven rack position for best results.) Remove from pans or baking sheets immediately. Cool on racks.

CHERRY NUT COFFEE BREAD

1 recipe CoolRise Sweet Dough
¾ c. cut-up maraschino cherries
1 c. chopped walnuts
Salad oil
1 (8 oz.) pkg. cream cheese, softened
½ c. sifted confectioners sugar

Make CoolRise Sweet Dough, but stir in cherries with wooden spoon after adding eggs and 1 c. flour and beating 1 minute at high speed.

When ready to shape, after punching down dough, divide in half. Roll 1 portion into a 20x6-inch rectangle on lightly buttered board. Cut lengthwise into 5 equal strips.

Shape into a 10x6-inch rectangle by placing first strip, cut edge down, on greased baking sheet or in a 15½x10½x1-inch jelly roll pan. Bring one end of strip around to start a second row. Join strips as you go, making rows 10 inches long. Tuck loose ends under. The completed coffee bread will look like ribbon candy.

Sprinkle with ½ c. of walnuts. Press together gently to make rows of dough stand up.

Repeat procedures with the remaining dough and walnuts. Brush with oil. Cover baking sheets loosely with plastic wrap. Refrigerate as recipe for CoolRise Sweet Dough directs.

Bake in 375° oven 25 to 30 minutes or until done. (Bake on lower rack position for best results.)

Remove from baking sheets immediately. Cool on racks. Combine cream cheese and confectioners sugar in bowl; stir until smooth. Frost cooled coffee breads. Serve remaining spread with coffee bread. Makes 2 coffee breads.

APRICOT COFFEE BREAD

¾ c. dried apricots
1½ c. water
⅓ c. sugar
½ tsp. ground ginger
1 recipe CoolRise Sweet Dough
Salad oil
Melted butter or regular margarine

Simmer apricots in water, uncovered, 20 to 30 minutes, or until tender. Drain; mash fruit well with fork. Add sugar and ginger; mix well. Cool.

When ready to shape CoolRise Sweet Dough, divide in half. Roll each half into a 14x9-inch rectangle on lightly greased board. Cut lengthwise into 3 equal strips.

Spread 2 tblsp. apricot mixture down center of each strip. Pinch lengthwise edges of strip together to form a rope.

Braid 3 ropes together on lightly greased baking sheet, starting at center and braiding to each end. Tuck ends under braid.

Repeat procedure with second half of dough and apricot mixture. Brush with oil. Cover loosely with plastic wrap. Refrigerate as above.

Bake in 375° oven 25 to 30 minutes or until done. (Bake on lower oven rack position for best results.) Remove from baking sheets immediately. Cool on racks. Brush while warm with melted butter. Frost when cool with your favorite confectioners sugar frosting or sprinkle with sifted confectioners sugar. Makes 2 coffee braids.

COOLRISE TWIRLS

1 recipe CoolRise Sweet Dough
Salad oil

Prepare CoolRise Sweet Dough as directed. When ready to shape, divide dough into 2 equal portions. Round up each portion into a ball.

Roll each portion into 15x12-inch rectangle on lightly greased board. Cut into 15 (1-inch) strips.

Twist each strip. Hold one end of twisted strip on lightly greased baking sheet and wind strip around this point. Tuck ends under. Place rolls several inches apart. Brush with oil. Cover loosely with plastic wrap. Refrigerate as above.

Bake in 375° oven 15 to 20 minutes, or until done. Remove from baking sheet immediately. Cool on racks.

Frost while warm with your favorite confectioners sugar frosting. Decorate as desired. Makes 30 rolls.

MEXICAN SWEET ROLLS

½ c. sugar
½ c. flour
½ tsp. ground cinnamon
⅓ c. finely chopped nuts
¼ c. melted butter or regular
  margarine
1 egg white, beaten until frothy
½ recipe CoolRise Sweet Dough
Salad oil

Combine sugar, flour, cinnamon, nuts, melted butter and egg white in bowl.

Prepare CoolRise Sweet Dough as recipe directs. When ready to shape, pinch off pieces of dough of equal size and shape into balls 1½ inches in diameter. Place on greased baking sheets about 3 inches apart. Press each ball down to flatten slightly.

With finger, make indentation in center of each ball. Top with spoonful of sugar-cinnamon mixture. Brush with oil. Cover loosely with plastic wrap. Refrigerate as above.

Bake in 375° oven 15 to 20 minutes or until done. Remove from baking sheets immediately. Cool on racks. Makes 18 rolls.

Guests just expect me to have Banana Bread in the freezer at all times. We like pecans rather than walnuts in the batter. I like to serve warm-from-the-oven Banana Bread with a big scoop of vanilla ice cream at our dessert bridges. (California) □This Banana Bread is my husband's absolute favorite recipe. He prefers peanut butter spread between two layers of Banana Bread to any meat sandwich—he carries this in his lunchbox at least three times a week. (Virginia)   □This recipe turns out an especially good banana loaf. I won first prize with the bread at the local county fair. (Oregon)

BANANA BREAD

3½ c. sifted flour
3 tsp. baking powder
1 tsp. salt
1 tsp. baking soda
2 c. mashed, ripe bananas
2 tblsp. lemon juice
¾ c. shortening
1½ c. sugar
3 eggs
¾ c. milk
½ c. chopped pecans or walnuts

Sift together flour, baking powder, salt and baking soda.

Combine bananas and lemon juice; mix well.

Cream together shortening and sugar in bowl with electric mixer at medium speed until fluffy. Add eggs and beat thoroughly until very light and fluffy. Add dry ingredients alternately with milk; fold in bananas and nuts. Beat after each addition. Pour into 2 greased 8½x4½x2½-inch loaf pans.

Bake in 350° oven 1 hour or until cake tester or wooden pick inserted in center of loaf comes out clean. Cool in pans 10 minutes. Remove from pans and cool on racks. Wrap in foil or plastic wrap and let stand in cool place overnight before slicing or freeze. Makes 2 loaves.

There's no doubt about it, Cinnamon Twist Bread is the most delicious bread I have ever made. Several years ago I baked 18 loaves for my sons to give to their teachers as Christmas gifts. Every teacher called and asked for the recipe. (Nebraska) □This bread is my standard hostess gift. I make and freeze eight loaves at a time. This still isn't enough to suit my family. (Idaho) □Every year I visit my daughter in New England. The first item I unpack is a loaf of Cinnamon Twist Bread. Everyone in the family has been looking forward to this special treat. (New York)

CINNAMON TWIST BREAD

1 c. milk, scalded
¼ c. shortening
½ c. sugar
2 tsp. salt
2 pkgs. active dry yeast
½ c. lukewarm water (110 to 115°)
6 c. sifted flour
2 eggs, slightly beaten
½ c. sugar
1 tblsp. ground cinnamon
1 tblsp. soft butter or regular
   margarine

Combine milk and shortening, ½ c. sugar and salt. Cool to lukewarm.

Sprinkle yeast on lukewarm water; stir to dissolve. Add yeast, 3 c. flour and eggs to milk mixture. Beat with electric mixer 2 minutes at medium speed, scraping bowl occasionally. Or beat by hand until batter sheets off spoon. Mix in enough remaining flour, a little at a time, to make a soft dough that leaves the sides of bowl. Turn out onto lightly floured board; knead until smooth, about 10 minutes. Place in lightly greased bowl; turn dough over to grease top. Cover and let rise in warm place until doubled, about 1½ hours.

Punch down; cover and let rise again until almost doubled, about 30 minutes. Turn onto board; divide in half. Round each half to make a ball. Cover and let rest 10 minutes.

Roll each half into a 12x7-inch rectangle. Combine ½ c. sugar and cinnamon; save out 1 tblsp. for topping. Sprinkle dough rectangles evenly with sugar-cinnamon mixture. Sprinkle 1 tsp. cold water over each rectangle. Spread smooth with spatula. Roll as for jelly roll, starting at narrow end. Seal along edge; tuck under ends. Place, sealed edge down, in 2 greased 9x5x3-inch loaf pans. Cover and let rise until almost doubled, 45 to 60 minutes.

Brush tops of loaves with soft butter and sprinkle with reserved sugar-cinnamon mixture.

Bake in 375° oven 35 to 40 minutes or until done. Remove from pans; cool on racks. Makes 2 loaves.

Butter Crescents were my first attempt at bread making. I made them for my husband's family reunion and he comes from a family of good bread bakers. My rolls were praised over and over again—now I have a reputation for being a fine bread maker. (Ohio) □I have been asked repeatedly for the Butter Crescent recipe. It has won many purple ribbons at fairs and I wouldn't dare show up at a potluck without a batch of these rolls. (Nebraska) □A gift that is always appreciated—a basket of these rolls along with a jar of my homemade strawberry freezer jam. (North Dakota)

BUTTER CRESCENTS

½ c. milk
½ c. butter or regular margarine
⅓ c. sugar
¾ tsp. salt
1 pkg. active dry yeast
½ c. lukewarm water (110 to 115°)
1 egg, beaten
4 c. sifted flour

Scald milk and pour over butter, sugar and salt in bowl. Cool to lukewarm.

Sprinkle yeast on lukewarm water; stir to dissolve.

Add egg, yeast and 2 c. flour to milk mixture. Beat with electric mixer at low speed until smooth, about 1 minute. Then beat at medium speed until thick, about 2 minutes.

Add enough remaining flour to make a dough that leaves the sides of bowl. Turn onto a lightly floured surface and knead gently. Put into a greased bowl; invert to grease top of dough. Cover and let rise in warm place until doubled, about 1 hour.

Turn dough onto lightly floured surface. Divide in half; cover and let rest 10 minutes. Roll each half to 12-inch circle; cut each circle in 12 wedges. Roll up each wedge from wide end and place pointed end down, on greased baking sheets. Curve ends slightly to make crescents (see variation). Cover and let rise until doubled, about 30 minutes.

Bake in 400° oven 15 minutes, changing position of baking sheets in oven when half baked. Remove from baking sheets and cool on racks. Makes 24 crescents.

Note: You can refrigerate the dough overnight before you let it rise. After kneading dough, place in lightly greased bowl and turn dough over to grease top. Cover with a piece of waxed paper, brushed with salad oil, and lay a piece of aluminum foil on top. Place in refrigerator. In the morning, let stand at room temperature until dough rises and is soft enough to roll, then turn dough onto board and proceed as with dough that was not refrigerated.

PEANUT BUTTER CRESCENTS

1 recipe Butter Crescents
⅓ c. peanut butter
⅓ c. honey
⅛ tsp. salt
½ tsp. ground cinnamon

Follow recipe for Butter Crescents, but before cutting the circles of dough and rolling the pie-shaped pieces, spread with the following mixture. Combine peanut butter and honey in bowl. Stir in salt and cinnamon; mix well. Proceed as directed for Butter Crescents.

These Square Doughnuts are so light and puffy that you almost have to tie them down. (Pennsylvania) ☐When my husband was a child he would visit a neighbor and demolish these doughnuts—he had never had them since until I tried your recipe. If I want them to last I have to hide them or plan to make another batch the next day. (California) ☐These doughnuts are handsome and look as if they are hard to make but they are so simple. (Minnesota) ☐A recipe for an outstanding home-made glazed doughnut is hard to find these days. My boys offer to help me glaze if I will agree to make a batch of Square Doughnuts every week. (Wisconsin)

SQUARE DOUGHNUTS

¾ c. milk
¼ c. sugar
1 tsp. salt
¼ c. butter or regular margarine
1 pkg. active dry yeast
¼ c. lukewarm water (110 to 115°)
1 egg, beaten
3¼ to 3½ c. unsifted flour
Cooking oil

Scald milk. Pour over sugar, salt and butter in bowl. Cool until lukewarm.

Sprinkle yeast on lukewarm water; stir to dissolve.

Add yeast, egg and half of the flour. Beat until smooth. Stir in enough of remaining flour to make a soft dough. For lightness, add only enough flour to make a dough you can handle.

Turn dough onto a lightly floured surface. Knead until smooth and elastic, about 5 to 10 minutes. (If dough sticks to the hands, grease them lightly with shortening or oil.)

Place dough in a greased bowl, then turn the bottom side up. Cover with damp cloth; let rise in a warm place until doubled, about 1 hour.

Punch down dough. On a lightly floured surface, roll about ½-inch thick to make a 12x10-inch rectangle. With a sharp knife, cut in 2½-inch squares (cut in rounds if you prefer round doughnuts); cut holes in centers with a 1-inch cutter or bottle top. Place doughnuts on oiled baking sheets or waxed paper, about 2 inches apart. Cover with inverted baking pans (allow room for dough to rise) or with a cloth. Let rise until doubled, about 1 hour.

About 15 minutes before end of rising period, heat oil in deep fryer or electric skillet to 375°.

Handle the doughnuts as gently as possible so they will not fall. Fry them, a few at a time, in deep oil 2 to 3 minutes, or until brown on both sides. Turn doughnuts only once. Drain on paper towels. While still warm, dip in a glaze or granulated sugar (recipes follow). Makes about 20 doughnuts.

Vanilla Glaze: Blend 2 c. sifted confectioners sugar, ⅓ c. milk and 1 tsp. vanilla. Dip warm doughnuts into glaze and drain them on a rack over waxed paper. Reuse the glaze that drips off.

Spicy Glaze: Make like Vanilla Glaze, but omit the vanilla and add ½ tsp. cinnamon and ¼ tsp. nutmeg.

Orange Glaze: Follow recipe for Vanilla Glaze, but omit vanilla and substitute orange juice for milk.

Every time I made doughnuts they were a flop—my husband told me not to bother to make doughnuts. I read your recipe for Puffy Potato Doughnuts and they sounded super and easy. Now my husband says I can make these anytime. (Iowa) □For bake sales, I put 12 doughnuts on a dowel, wrap them in clear plastic film and tie with red yarn. We sell as many dozen as I can make. (Nebraska) □Made a batch of Puffy Doughnuts and gave to my father-in-law for Father's Day. As soon as they were gone, he phoned and said he wouldn't mind having another batch real soon. (Montana)

PUFFY POTATO DOUGHNUTS

2 c. milk
½ c. butter or regular margarine
1 c. sugar
1 tblsp. salt
1 pkg. active dry yeast
1 tsp. sugar
¼ c. lukewarm water (110 to 115°)
1 tsp. baking powder
½ tsp. baking soda
1 c. unseasoned mashed potatoes
3 egg yolks
8 c. sifted flour
Cooking oil
Vanilla Glaze (recipe follows)

Scald milk. Pour over butter, 1 c. sugar and salt in bowl. Cool to lukewarm.

Sprinkle yeast and 1 tsp. sugar on lukewarm water; stir to dissolve. Add yeast, baking powder, baking soda, mashed potatoes, egg yolks and 2 c. flour to milk mixture. Beat with electric mixer at medium speed until smooth, about 2 minutes, scraping bowl occasionally. Or beat with spoon until batter is smooth.

Gradually add remaining flour, blending well. (Dough will be soft.) Place in lightly greased bowl; turn dough over to grease top. Cover and let rise in warm place until doubled, about 2 hours.

Roll out dough ¼-inch thick on floured surface. Cut with floured doughnut cutter. Place on floured waxed paper. Cover and let rise until doubled, about 1 hour.

Fry a few doughnuts at a time in hot cooking oil (350°) until golden brown, turning once. Drain on paper towels. Coat warm doughnuts with Vanilla Glaze. Place on cooling rack to dry. Makes about 3½ dozen.

VANILLA GLAZE

1 lb. box confectioners sugar
½ c. soft butter or regular margarine
7 tblsp. milk or light cream
2½ tsp. vanilla

Combine confectioners sugar, butter, milk and vanilla in bowl. Beat until smooth.

My family can hardly wait until these Raised Doughnuts are glazed and cooled. I always double the recipe. (New York) □I have always wanted a good glazed doughnut recipe and this is a dandy. These beauties have traveled through two counties. Many friends have suggested I open a shop and sell only these doughnuts. (Indiana) □For several years, I worked as a cook for the U.S. Forest Service. I quadrupled the recipe twice a week and the rangers stood in line whenever they knew I was frying doughnuts. We renamed them Spotted Bear Doughnuts. Never found a man who could stop before he had eaten at least three of these doughnuts. (Montana)

RAISED DOUGHNUTS

¾ c. milk
⅓ c. sugar
1 tsp. salt
1 pkg. active dry yeast
¼ c. lukewarm water (110 to 115°)
4¼ c. sifted flour
1 tsp. ground nutmeg
⅓ c. soft shortening
2 eggs
Cooking oil

Scald milk. Pour over sugar and salt in bowl. Cool to lukewarm.

Sprinkle yeast over lukewarm water; stir until dissolved. Add yeast, 2 c. flour and nutmeg to milk mixture. Beat well. Stir in shortening, then eggs.

Add remaining flour, kneading in last portion on lightly floured surface.

Place in greased bowl, turning once to grease top. Let rise in warm place until doubled.

Turn out on floured board. Roll dough ⅓-inch thick; cut with doughnut cutter. Remove trimmings and form into ball. When doubled, roll out and cut. Or make Pecan Rolls (recipe follows).

Let cut doughnuts rise until very light (30 to 40 minutes). Leave uncovered so crust will form.

Pick up doughnuts on floured wide spatula and ease into deep hot oil (375°). Fry until golden brown, turning once. Drain on paper towels. Makes 2 dozen.

Sugared Doughnuts: While doughnuts are still warm, dip into bowl of granulated sugar or mixture of sugar and cinnamon (½ c. sugar to ½ tsp. cinnamon). Or, when doughnuts have cooled, shake in bag containing confectioners sugar.

Glazed Doughnuts: Mix 1½ c. sifted confectioners sugar with enough boiling water (about 3 tblsp.) to make thin glaze. Dip slightly cooled doughnuts into warm glaze. Cool on cake rack with piece of waxed paper underneath.

Raised Orange Doughnuts: Proceed as for raised doughnuts. In place of milk use ½ c. orange juice plus ¼ c. boiling water. Use 2 tblsp. finely grated orange rind instead of nutmeg.

Pecan Rolls from Doughnut Centers: Lightly grease 6 (2½-inch) muffin-pan cups. Place 1 tsp. brown sugar, 1 tsp. light corn syrup, ½ tsp. water, 3 pecan halves and 3 raisins in each. Arrange 4 doughnut centers on top. Cover and let rise in warm place until doubled, about 30 minutes. Bake in 350° oven 25 to 30 minutes or until golden. Makes 6 rolls.

CoolRise French Bread lets me serve my family homemade bread during the hottest summer months. I bake it early in the morning. It has such a good flavor, plain or toasted. All of my friends who have tasted this now make their own bread using this recipe. (Indiana)   □I make this the night before my guests arrive and bake it an hour before they appear at the door—then they can smell that wonderful odor of homemade bread as they walk in. Never fails to bring "ohs" and "ahs" of delight. (New Jersey)   □An easy bread to make, with a chewy crust and soft texture—just the way we like it. I serve it often with a big pot of homemade soup or stew for supper. (New York)

COOLRISE FRENCH BREAD

5½ to 6½ c. sifted flour
2 pkgs. active dry yeast
1 tblsp. sugar
1 tblsp. salt
2 tblsp. softened butter or regular
   margarine
2¼ c. hot water (120 to 130°)
Cooking oil

Combine 2 c. flour, undissolved yeast, sugar and salt in large bowl. Stir well to blend. Add butter. Add hot water to ingredients in bowl all at once. Beat with electric mixer at medium speed 2 minutes. Scrape bowl occasionally.

Add 1 c. more flour. Beat with electric mixer at high speed 1 minute or until thick and elastic. Scrape bowl occasionally.

Gradually stir in just enough of remaining flour with wooden spoon to make a soft dough that leaves the sides of bowl. Turn out on floured board. Round up to make a ball.

Knead 5 to 10 minutes or until dough is smooth and elastic. Cover with plastic wrap, then with towel. Let rest 20 minutes on board. Punch down.

Divide dough into 2 equal portions.

Roll each portion into 15x8-inch rectangle on

lightly greased board. Roll up tightly like jelly roll, beginning with long side. Seal lengthwise edge and ends well. Tuck ends under. Taper ends by rolling gently with hand. Place, seam side down, on greased baking sheets. Brush lightly with oil. Cover baking sheets loosely with plastic wrap.

Refrigerate 2 to 24 hours at moderately cold setting. When ready to bake, remove from refrigerator. Uncover. Let stand 10 minutes while preheating oven. Brush gently with cold water. Slash tops of loaves diagonally at 2-inch intervals with sharp knife just before baking.

Bake in 400° oven 30 to 40 minutes or until done. Remove from baking sheets immediately. Cool on racks. Makes 2 long loaves.

There was an overflow of zucchini in my garden—so I tried your recipe for Zucchini Nut Bread. It was a huge success with my family. The kids like it for an after-school snack as well as in their lunchboxes. I found by putting the zucchini in my blender, instead of grating it, I saved a lot of time. (Minnesota) □This bread makes lovely party sandwiches when sliced thin and spread with cream cheese. (Alabama) □A moist quick bread that goes well with meals or served as a dessert with a dish of fresh fruit. (New York) □A great-textured bread—I make and freeze many loaves of this in the summer. Serve year-round with coffee to neighbors and friends. The recipe has been passed along to lots of people. (California)

ZUCCHINI NUT BREAD

3 c. sifted flour
1½ tsp. ground cinnamon
1 tsp. baking soda
1 tsp. salt
¼ tsp. baking powder
3 eggs
2 c. sugar
1 c. cooking oil
1 tblsp. vanilla
2 c. grated, unpared zucchini squash
½ c. chopped walnuts
1 tsp. flour

Sift together 3 c. flour, cinnamon, baking soda, salt and baking powder.

Beat eggs well in bowl. Gradually add sugar and oil, mixing well. Add vanilla and dry ingredients; blend well. Stir in zucchini.

Combine walnuts with 1 tsp. flour; stir into batter. Pour into 2 greased 8½x4½x2½-inch loaf pans.

Bake in 350° oven 1 hour or until bread tests done. Cool in pans on racks 10 minutes. Remove from pans; cool on racks. Makes 2 loaves.

Refrigerator Bran Muffins—an excellent recipe for a busy farm wife. (Minnesota) ☐I've shared this recipe so many times. Everyone likes these muffins and it's so handy to have the batter ready to use in the refrigerator. (Missouri) ☐These muffins complement any meal. For variety, I add raisins or coconut. (Kansas) ☐My husband likes homemade hot bread for breakfast. These bran muffins are the only recipe I have time to fix. I keep a container of Bran Muffin Batter in the refrigerator all winter long. (Ohio) ☐I like recipes that are nutritious. These muffins have lots of vitamins, minerals, protein and fiber—plus tasting divine. (Iowa)

REFRIGERATOR BRAN MUFFINS

5 c. sifted flour
5 tsp. baking soda
2 tsp. salt
2 c. boiling water
2 c. whole bran cereal
2 c. sugar
1 c. shortening
4 eggs, well beaten
1 qt. buttermilk
4 c. whole bran cereal buds

Sift together flour, baking soda and salt.

Pour boiling water over whole bran cereal; set aside.

Cream together sugar and shortening in 6-qt. bowl until light. Add eggs and beat well. Blend in buttermilk, bran buds and the soaked whole bran cereal. Add sifted dry ingredients; mix well. Store in tightly covered container in refrigerator. Batter will keep up to 6 weeks.

To make muffins, fill greased muffin-pan cups two-thirds full. Bake in 400° oven about 20 minutes. Makes 5 dozen muffins.

Sugar-Top Coffee Cake—so good with a cup of freshly brewed coffee. (Montana) □My favorite method of entertaining is a late morning brunch—my favorite cake to serve at these affairs is your Sugar-Top Coffee Cake along with a cheese souffle. (Idaho) □When I served this coffee cake to several friends, one thought it was a yeast coffee cake and the other said she hadn't tasted anything so good for many a year and promptly wrote down the recipe. (Florida)

SUGAR-TOP COFFEE CAKE

1 egg
¾ c. sugar
1 tblsp. melted butter or regular
   margarine
1 c. dairy sour cream
1 tsp. vanilla
1½ c. sifted flour
2 tsp. baking powder
¼ tsp. baking soda
¾ tsp. salt
½ c. brown sugar, firmly packed
2 tblsp. flour
½ tsp. ground cinnamon
2 tblsp. softened butter or regular
   margarine

Beat egg in bowl with electric mixer at medium speed until frothy. Add sugar and 1 tblsp. butter, beating until light and fluffy. Add sour cream and vanilla; blend well.

Sift together 1½ c. flour, baking powder, baking soda and salt. Stir into sour cream mixture; blend well. Pour into greased 8-inch square baking pan.

Combine brown sugar, 2 tblsp. flour, cinnamon and 2 tblsp. butter into bowl; mix until crumbly. Sprinkle over batter.

Bake in 375° oven 25 to 30 minutes or until done. Serve warm. Makes 6 servings.

CAKES, FROSTINGS & FILLINGS

CAKES, FROSTINGS & FILLINGS

APPLESAUCE FRUITCAKE
FUDGE CAKE
NOBBY APPLE CAKE
FRUITCAKE
14-CARAT CAKE
BLUE RIBBON BANANA CAKE
BROWN MOUNTAIN CAKE
CARROT/PECAN SPICE CAKE
PUMPKIN CAKE
MARBLED POUND CAKE
SHENANDOAH VALLEY APPLE CAKE
ROCKY MOUNTAIN CAKE
SPICY PRUNE CAKE
FROZEN CAKE ROLL, FOUR WAYS
GRAND CHAMPION SPONGE CAKE
LEMON SUNSHINE CAKE
YELLOW LARD CAKE
GINGERBREAD DELUXE
BLACK WALNUT CAKE
LEMON CHEESE CAKE
SOUR CREAM POUND CAKE
BOILED RAISIN CAKE
COCOA CHIFFON CAKE
CHAMPION ANGEL FOOD CAKE
CHOCOLATE NUT LOAF

First-Choice Cakes

Of the hundreds of cakes published in our cookbooks, it was no surprise to have our elegant Fudge Cake outrank all the rest. This velvety, tender-crumbed three-layer cake has an emphatically chocolate taste and an unusual creamy date filling. Like many of the favorites in this category, it's a towering special-occasion cake. But women also wrote about the good old-fashioned homey cakes they bake in square or oblong pans—these seem to be special favorites of the men. Shenandoah Valley Apple Cake and Spicy Prune Cake are examples of these hearty, moist, down-to-earth cakes. Farm women cut them in generous squares to eat out of hand, to pack in lunchboxes or to serve a hungry field crew.

Many of the choices reflected the bounty of gardens and orchards—a farm wife's delight in discovering a recipe to help use plentiful home-grown apples, pumpkins, black walnuts and even carrots. Applesauce Fruitcake and Nobby Apple Cake followed Fudge Cake as second and third choices in the cake category. Carrot Pecan Spice Cake and 14-Carat Cake, both using carrots, also were near the top, and are Thanksgiving specialties along with pumpkin and mince pies in many farm homes. All four are mentioned many times as great fall favorites to take to church suppers and bake sales.

Women who nominated the many elegant layer cakes and tube cakes were remembering moments of triumph—often a well-deserved blue ribbon at the fair. Grand Champion Sponge, Blue Ribbon Banana and Rocky Mountain Cake have all taken prizes; they've also been the center of attention at birthday parties and other special occasions.

Certain cakes—Boiled Raisin, or Lemon Cheese Cake—made this list because they're reminiscent of the cakes talked about in family histories—great-grandmothers' heritage cakes. Other women wrote about traditions of their own making—how FARM JOURNAL'S Fruitcake is now a featured part of their Christmas baking and giving each holiday season.

We think you will enjoy making all these cakes from plain to fancy—perhaps they will become *your* special-occasion cake or blue ribbon winner.

Making Applesauce Fruitcake is a Christmas tradition with our family. We bake the batter in various size cans and metal bowls to give as gift cakes in a variety of shapes. (Wisconsin) □When our children can't come home for Christmas, they ask me to send them an Applesauce Fruitcake—it's a taste of home, they tell me. (Ohio) □My husband's very favorite cake. I bake and freeze at least four batches so we can eat the cake year round. (Indiana) □ Many of our friends never liked fruitcake until they tasted this one. (Pennsylvania)

APPLESAUCE FRUITCAKE

3 c. applesauce
1 c. shortening
2 c. sugar
1 lb. dates, pitted and chopped
1 lb. raisins
1 lb. walnuts, coarsely chopped
¼ lb. candied cherries, quartered
¼ lb. candied pineapple, chopped
¼ lb. citron, finely chopped
4½ c. sifted flour
4 tsp. baking soda
2½ tsp. ground cinnamon
1 tsp. salt
1 tsp. ground nutmeg
½ tsp. ground cloves
½ c. light corn syrup
¼ c. water
Candied fruit and nuts

Combine applesauce, shortening and sugar in 2-qt. saucepan; mix well. Boil 5 minutes, stirring occasionally. Cool well.

Place dates, raisins, walnuts, cherries, pineapple and citron in 6-qt. bowl.

Sift together flour, baking soda, cinnamon, salt, nutmeg and cloves over fruit mixture. Mix until all fruit is well coated. Stir in cooled applesauce mixture; mix well. Turn into 4 greased and waxed paper-lined 1 lb. coffee cans. Or use four 7½x3½x2½-

inch loaf pans. (Recipe makes 12 c. batter.)

Bake in 250° oven 2 hours 30 minutes or until cakes test done. Cool in pans on racks 10 minutes. Remove from pans; cool on racks. Store in a moisture-proof wrap in a cool place or freeze.

Let mellow at least 2 weeks before cutting. Glaze loaves before cutting. Combine corn syrup and water in saucepan. Bring to a boil. Remove from heat and cool to lukewarm. Pour over loaves. Decorate with candied fruit and nuts. Makes 4 cakes.

This Fudge Cake truly deserves its five stars—the very best cake I have ever eaten. (Iowa) □My mother won 20 blue ribbons with this cake and I've won six so far. My husband and three sons insist on Fudge Cake for their birthdays—no other cake will do. (Nebraska) □We serve this cake on very special occasions. I believe it's the rich fudge frosting and creamy date filling that makes it so different from any other chocolate cake. (Oklahoma) □A top favorite with my family. It has traveled to picnics, reunions, church suppers, weddings and showers—outshines any cake in existence. (Pennsylvania) □I make this cake in a jelly roll pan and top with a broiled icing. (Virginia)

FUDGE CAKE

¾ c. butter or regular margarine
2¼ c. sugar
1½ tsp. vanilla
3 eggs
3 (1 oz.) squares unsweetened
    chocolate, melted
3 c. sifted cake flour
1½ tsp. baking soda
¾ tsp. salt
1½ c. ice water
Date Cream Filling (recipe follows)
Fudge Frosting (recipe follows)

Cream together butter and sugar in mixing bowl until light and fluffy at medium speed of electric mixer. Beat in vanilla. Add eggs, one at a time, beating well after each addition. Blend in chocolate.

Sift together cake flour, baking soda and salt. Add dry ingredients alternately with water to creamed mixture, beating well after each addition. Pour batter into 3 greased and waxed paper-lined 8-inch round cake pans.

Bake in 350° oven 30 to 35 minutes or until cake tests done. Cool in pans on racks 10 minutes. Remove from pans; cool on racks.

Prepare Date Cream Filling. Spread between layers. Prepare Fudge Frosting. Spread on sides and top of cake. Makes 12 servings.

DATE CREAM FILLING

1 c. milk
½ c. chopped dates
1 tblsp. flour
¼ c. sugar
1 egg, beaten
½ c. chopped walnuts
1 tsp. vanilla

Combine milk and dates in top of double boiler. Heat mixture over low heat. Combine flour and sugar in small bowl. Add egg; beat until smooth. Stir into hot milk mixture; place over simmering water. Cook, stirring constantly, until thick. Cool. Stir in walnuts and vanilla.

FUDGE FROSTING

2 c. sugar
¼ tsp. salt
1 c. light cream
2 tblsp. light corn syrup
2 (1 oz.) squares unsweetened
    chocolate

Combine all ingredients in 2-qt. saucepan. Cook over low heat, stirring constantly, until sugar dissolves. Cover saucepan; cook 2 minutes. Remove cover and cook to 234° (soft ball stage). Remove from heat. Beat with wooden spoon to spreading consistency. Add a little hot water if frosting becomes too stiff or confectioners sugar if it becomes too thin.

Fudge Cake—recipe, page 186

Fruitcake—recipe, page 190

188

A great dessert on a crisp fall evening—Nobby Apple Cake is truly a distinctive cake to serve to guests. I often double the recipe to serve a crowd. (Oregon)   □Since we have lots of apple trees I'm always looking for new ways to use up all those apples—men love this. (South Dakota)   □Makes a big hit with my husband and the field crew at harvesttime. (Iowa)   □I serve this yummy apple cake warm from the oven with a scoop of vanilla ice cream for a nutritious snack before the evening milking. (Maryland)   □This is the only cake my husband likes without frosting. (Wisconsin)   □I make this often during summer and fall months and always double the recipe as one cake never lasts through the day. (Oregon)

NOBBY APPLE CAKE

3 tblsp. butter or regular margarine
1 c. sugar
1 egg
1 c. sifted flour
1 tsp. baking soda
½ tsp. salt
½ tsp. ground cinnamon
½ tsp. ground nutmeg
3 c. diced pared apples
¼ c. chopped walnuts
1 tsp. vanilla

Cream together butter and sugar in mixing bowl until light and fluffy at medium speed of electric mixer. Add egg; beat well.

Sift together flour, baking soda, salt, cinnamon and nutmeg. Add to creamed mixture; mixing well. (Batter is very stiff.) Add apples, walnuts and vanilla. Stir well with spoon until liquid is pressed out of apples and mixture looks like a thick cake batter. Turn into greased 8-inch square baking pan.

Bake in 350° oven 40 minutes or until cake tests done. Cool in pan on rack. Cake is delicious served either warm or cold. Makes 9 servings.

I do like the use of whole fruits and nuts in your Fruitcake—saves all that chopping time. (Iowa) □Every year I bake many batches for the holidays. Most are given as gifts but I save one for the family. In our area it's known as Jean's Cake. (Oregon) □Right after Thanksgiving I start baking this Fruitcake. I put the batter into little paper bonbon cups and include a few in every box of cookies I give as Christmas gifts. (Ohio) □This is the prettiest fruitcake after it's cut—the recipe is used throughout our area during the holidays. I am proud to say it is FARM JOURNAL'S recipe. (Minnesota)

FRUITCAKE

1 lb. mixed candied fruit (2 c.)
1 lb. whole dates, pitted
½ lb. whole candied cherries (1 c.)
¼ lb. chopped citron
1 c. raisins
1 c. pecan halves
1 c. walnut halves
4 c. sifted flour
1 tsp. salt
1 tsp. ground cinnamon
1 tsp. ground cloves
½ tsp. ground nutmeg
1 c. butter or regular margarine
2 c. sugar
4 eggs
1 tsp. baking soda
1½ c. buttermilk
Orange juice or apple cider

Prepare baking pans by cutting parchment or brown paper liners for bottoms. Grease each piece of paper with shortening. Place in pans. Top with a layer of waxed paper. Grease top of paper and inside of pans generously with shortening.

Place candied fruit, dates, cherries, citron, raisins, pecan and walnut halves in 6-qt. bowl.

Sift together flour, salt, cinnamon, cloves and nutmeg; reserve ½ c. Add reserved dry ingredients to fruit/nut mixture; mix to coat.

Cream together butter and sugar in bowl until light and fluffy at medium speed of electric mixer. Add eggs, one at a time, beating well after each addition. Add baking soda to dry ingredients. Add dry ingredients alternately with buttermilk to creamed mixture, beating well after each addition. Add batter to fruit/nut mixture, mixing well. Turn into prepared 10-inch tube pan or three 8½x4½x2½-inch loaf pans. To decorate, place fruits and walnuts on top of batter to form a design.

Bake in 300° oven 2 hours 30 minutes for 10-inch tube pan and 1 hour 30 minutes for loaf pans. Cool in pans on racks 10 minutes. Remove from pans; cool on racks. Baste with orange juice or apple cider using pastry brush. Wrap in waxed paper; then in aluminum foil. Store in covered container in cool place. Let mellow 2 weeks, then baste again. Makes 1 (10-inch) tube cake or 3 loaves.

I'll bet anything this 14-Carat Cake is a top favorite with all women—it's undoubtedly the very best cake of all. (Colorado) □I have tried many recipes for carrot cakes but none as good as this one. I always take this cake to our Church Homecoming and everyone always knows it's my cake. Needless to say every crumb disappears, and I mean every crumb. (Virginia) □So easy to make and my friends think it's the best carrot cake in the world—the canned pineapple in it makes the difference. (Kentucky) □Whenever I serve this cake to guests, they can't believe there are carrots in it—has such a lovely nutty flavor and keeps so well. (Illinois)

14-CARAT CAKE

2 c. sifted flour
2 tsp. baking powder
1½ tsp. baking soda
1½ tsp. salt
2 tsp. ground cinnamon
2 c. sugar
1½ c. salad oil
4 eggs
2 c. finely shredded pared carrots
1 (8½ oz.) can crushed pineapple,
   drained
½ c. chopped walnuts
1 (3½ oz.) can flaked
   coconut
Cream Cheese Frosting (recipe
   follows)

Sift together flour, baking powder, baking soda, salt and cinnamon in mixing bowl. Add sugar, oil and eggs. Beat at medium speed of electric mixer 1 minute. Stir in carrots, pineapple, walnuts and coconut. Turn into 3 greased and floured 9-inch round cake pans.

Bake in 350° oven 40 minutes or until cakes test done. Cool in pans on racks 10 minutes. Remove from pans; cool on racks.

Prepare Cream Cheese Frosting. Fill layers and frost top and sides of cake. Makes 12 servings.

CREAM CHEESE FROSTING

½ c. butter or regular margarine
1 (8 oz.) pkg. cream cheese, softened
1 tsp. vanilla
1 (1 lb.) box confectioners sugar

Cream together butter, cream cheese and vanilla in bowl at medium speed of electric mixer. Gradually add confectioners sugar, beating well until smooth and creamy. If mixture is too thick to spread, add a little milk.

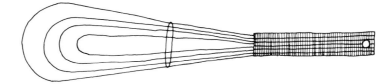

Blue Ribbon Banana Cake is well-named. It's won seven blue ribbons for me. (Kansas) □This is our favorite birthday cake for adults. It's so handsome we never clutter it with candles. (Washington) □This is my most requested cake when my husband's family come to visit. Popular at our church picnics, too. (Virginia) □So elegant to serve and so easy to make. I often make two cakes when bananas are a bargain—one to eat and one to freeze. (Illinois) □Scrumptious describes this cake—I use freshly grated coconut instead of the canned. (Michigan)

BLUE RIBBON BANANA CAKE

¾ c. shortening
1½ c. sugar
2 eggs
1 c. mashed bananas
2 c. sifted flour
1 tsp. baking soda
1 tsp. baking powder
½ tsp. salt
½ c. buttermilk
1 tsp. vanilla
½ c. chopped pecans
1 c. flaked coconut
Creamy Nut Filling (recipe follows)
White Snow Frosting (recipe follows)

Cream together shortening and sugar in mixing bowl until light and fluffy at medium speed of electric mixer. Add eggs; beat 2 more minutes. Add bananas; beat 2 more minutes.

Sift together flour, baking soda, baking powder and salt. Add dry ingredients alternately with buttermilk to creamed mixture, beating well after each addition. Add vanilla; beat 2 minutes. Stir in pecans. Turn into 2 greased and floured 9-inch round cake pans. Sprinkle ½ c. coconut on each layer.

Bake in 375° oven 25 to 30 minutes or until cakes test done. Cool in pans on racks 10 minutes. Remove from pans; cool on racks.

Prepare Creamy Nut Filling. Place first layer coconut side down on plate and spread with Creamy Nut Filling. Top with second layer, coconut side up. Prepare White Snow Frosting. Swirl frosting around sides and about 1-inch around top edge, leaving center unfrosted. Makes 12 servings.

CREAMY NUT FILLING

½ c. sugar
2 tblsp. flour
½ c. light cream
2 tblsp. butter or regular margarine
½ c. chopped pecans
¼ tsp. salt
1 tsp. vanilla

Combine sugar, flour, light cream and butter in heavy 2-qt. saucepan. Cook, stirring constantly, until thickened. Stir in pecans, salt and vanilla. Cool.

WHITE SNOW FROSTING

1 egg white
¼ c. shortening
¼ c. butter or regular margarine
½ tsp. coconut extract
½ tsp. vanilla
2 c. sifted confectioners sugar

Cream together egg white, shortening, butter, coconut extract and vanilla in bowl at medium speed of electric mixer. Gradually add confectioners sugar, beating until light and fluffy.

Brown Mountain Cake has a delicate chocolate flavor. And in our family we prefer the gentler chocolate taste. The frosting stays soft and creamy. (North Dakota) □This cake has traveled to ice cream socials, picnics and birthday parties and it's always a big hit. (Illinois) □Often, I pour the batter into cupcake pans and bake. Then I frost each cupcake and dip it into chopped nuts. Try to keep at least a dozen in the freezer to serve unexpected guests. (New Mexico) □This cake whips up fast and disappears just as fast. (Wisconsin) □Have used this recipe to make a Wedding Cake several times—crumbs never mix into the frosting and the flavor is superb. (California)

BROWN MOUNTAIN CAKE

1 c. soft butter or regular margarine
2 c. sugar
3 eggs
3 c. sifted flour
1 tsp. baking soda
½ tsp. salt
3 tblsp. baking cocoa
1 c. buttermilk
1 tsp. vanilla
½ c. warm water
Chocolate Fudge Frosting
   (recipe follows)

Cream together butter and sugar in mixing bowl until light and fluffy at medium speed of electric mixer. Add eggs, one at a time, beating well after each addition.

Sift together flour, baking soda, salt and cocoa. Add dry ingredients alternately with buttermilk to creamed mixture, beating well after each addition. Beat in vanilla and water. Pour batter into greased and floured 13x9x2-inch baking pan.

Bake in 350° oven 45 minutes or until cake tests done. Cool in pan on rack.

Prepare Chocolate Fudge Frosting. Swirl on cake. Makes 16 servings.

CHOCOLATE FUDGE FROSTING

**2 (1 oz.) squares unsweetened
   chocolate
1½ c. sugar
1½ tblsp. light corn syrup
⅛ tsp. salt
½ c. milk
½ c. butter or regular margarine
1 tsp. vanilla**

Combine chocolate, sugar, corn syrup, salt and milk in 2-qt. saucepan. Cook over low heat, stirring constantly, until sugar dissolves and chocolate melts. Bring to a boil over medium heat, stirring occasionally. Reduce heat to low and simmer, without stirring, to 234° (soft ball stage). Remove from heat; add butter and cool to lukewarm (110°) without stirring. Add vanilla and beat at medium speed with electric mixer until frosting is creamy and barely holds its shape. Do not overbeat.

I love a fruitcake for the holidays but my family doesn't care for it. Carrot/Pecan Spice Cake is a happy compromise. (New York)   □This is my special cake that always goes to calf brandings. I bake it in a loaf pan—easier to carry. I take the orange glaze in a jar and pour it on just before serving. It's a favorite with the cowboys and their wives. (California)   □ This is the most popular cake at our monthly community potluck suppers. Never a crumb to take home. (Missouri)   □Carrot Pecan was the wedding cake at our grandson's dinner at his special request. We like to frost it with cream cheese frosting and decorate with pecan halves. (Utah)

CARROT/PECAN SPICE CAKE

1¼ c. salad oil
2 c. sugar
2 c. sifted flour
2 tsp. baking powder
1 tsp. baking soda
1 tsp. salt
2 tsp. ground cinnamon
4 eggs
3 c. grated pared carrots
1 c. finely chopped pecans
Orange Glaze (recipe follows)

Combine oil and sugar in mixing bowl. Beat well at medium speed of electric mixer.

Sift together flour, baking powder, baking soda, salt and cinnamon. Add half of dry ingredients to oil mixture; blend well. Add remaining dry ingredients alternately with eggs, one at a time, beating well after each addition. Stir in carrots and pecans. Pour batter into lightly oiled 10-inch tube pan.

Bake in 350° oven 1 hour 10 minutes or until cake tests done. Cool in pan on rack 10 minutes. Remove from pan; cool on rack.

Prepare Orange Glaze. Split cake in 3 horizontal layers. Spread Orange Glaze between layers and on top and sides of cake. Makes 12 servings.

ORANGE GLAZE

1 c. sugar
¼ c. cornstarch
1 c. orange juice
1 tsp. lemon juice
2 tblsp. butter or regular margarine
2 tblsp. grated orange rind
½ tsp. salt

Combine sugar and cornstarch in saucepan. Slowly stir in orange juice and lemon juice; mix until smooth. Add butter, orange rind and salt. Cook over low heat, stirring constantly, until thick and glossy. Cool well.

We raise pumpkins so I make Pumpkin Cake several times a week in the fall. I like to freeze some ahead for the football season. Our guests look forward to a big slice of this cake with hot cider when they gather at our house after a game. (Kansas) ☐No one can guess there's pumpkin in this cake—it has a unique flavor. (Missouri) ☐Pumpkin Cake has become a traditional birthday cake for my daughter's Halloween birthday. I bake cakes to make extra money and get many requests for Pumpkin Cake from my customers. (Indiana) ☐I like to make this nutritious cake for my youngsters as it uses eggs and pumpkin. (Wisconsin)

PUMPKIN CAKE

½ c. shortening
1 c. sugar
1 c. brown sugar, firmly packed
2 eggs
1 c. cooked, mashed or
   canned pumpkin
3 c. sifted cake flour
4 tsp. baking powder
¼ tsp. baking soda
½ c. milk
1 c. chopped walnuts
1 tsp. maple flavoring
Harvest Moon Frosting (recipe
   follows)

Cream together shortening and sugars in mixing bowl until light and fluffy at medium speed of electric mixer.

Add eggs and pumpkin, beating well.

Sift together cake flour, baking powder and baking soda. Add dry ingredients alternately with milk to creamed mixture, beating well after each addition. Stir in walnuts and maple flavoring. Pour batter into 3 greased 8-inch round cake pans.

Bake in 350° oven 30 minutes or until cakes test done. Cool in pans on racks 10 minutes. Remove from pans; cool on racks.

Prepare Harvest Moon Frosting. Spread frosting between layers. Frost sides and top of cake. Makes 12 servings.

HARVEST MOON FROSTING

3 egg whites
1½ c. brown sugar, firmly packed
6 tblsp. water
1 tsp. vanilla

Combine egg whites, brown sugar and water in top of double boiler. Beat well at high speed with electric mixer. Place over simmering water. Beat at high speed for 7 minutes or until soft peaks form. Remove from heat; blend in vanilla. Beat until thick enough to spread.

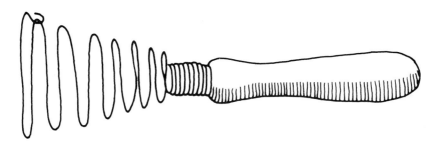

My grandchildren call your Marbled Pound Cake the Imagination Cake. They find all kinds of images and creations in the swirled patterns—it's their favorite cake when they visit Grandma. (Kansas)   □An especially handsome cake when made in a fluted tube pan. When I served it at a men's club meeting, many of the wives called me for the recipe—their husbands had raved about the cake. (Minnesota)   □For special occasions, I make the cake in three loaf pans. Slice each cake into five layers. Frost and fill with a chocolate frosting and decorate with chopped nuts and halved maraschino cherries. (Indiana)

MARBLED POUND CAKE

1¼ c. soft butter
2½ c. sugar
5 eggs
2 tsp. vanilla
2½ c. sifted flour
1¼ tsp. baking powder
½ tsp. salt
1 c. less 2 tblsp. milk
¼ c. baking cocoa

Cream together butter and sugar in large bowl until light and fluffy at medium speed of electric mixer. Add eggs, one at a time, beating well after each addition. Beat in vanilla.

Sift together flour, baking powder and salt. Add dry ingredients alternately with milk to creamed mixture, beating well. Remove 2 c. batter; add cocoa and blend well. Spoon a layer of white batter in greased and floured 10-inch tube pan or 10-inch fluted tube pan. Top with spoonfuls of chocolate batter. Alternate with white batter until all batter is used. Swirl with spatula to create marbled look.

Bake in 325° oven 1 hour 10 minutes for tube pan and 1 hour 30 minutes for fluted tube pan or until cake tests done. Cool in pan on rack 10 minutes. Remove from pan; cool on rack. Makes 12 servings.

The men who helped us build an addition to our barn voted Shenandoah Valley Apple Cake the best of all the cakes I served them. I would imagine it keeps well—haven't been able to keep it long enough to find out. (Kansas) □Just a wonderful homey cake that tastes so good warm from the oven. I make this often during harvesting season—it's a hearty cake that is always a favorite with our field crew. (Iowa) □Every year we have a bounty of apples from our trees—the children know they will find their favorite Shenandoah cake in their lunchboxes. (South Dakota)

SHENANDOAH VALLEY APPLE CAKE

1 c. cooking oil
2 c. sugar
3 eggs
1¼ tsp. vanilla
2 c. sifted flour
1 tsp. salt
1 tsp. baking soda
3 c. diced pared apples
1 c. chopped walnuts
1 tblsp. flour
½ c. butter or regular margarine
1 c. brown sugar, firmly packed
¼ c. milk

Beat oil, sugar, eggs and vanilla in bowl at medium speed of electric mixer (about 3 minutes).

Sift together 2 c. flour, salt and baking soda. Gradually add dry ingredients to egg mixture, beating well after each addition. Stir in apples. Combine walnuts and 1 tblsp. flour; add to batter. Pour into greased and floured 13x9x2-inch baking pan.

Bake in 350° oven 1 hour or until cake tests done. Cool in pan on rack.

Combine butter, brown sugar and milk in saucepan. Cook over medium heat, stirring constantly, until mixture boils. Boil 3 minutes. Remove from heat; spread at once on cake. Makes 16 servings.

Was I ever thrilled when my niece won her first blue ribbon with Rocky Mountain Cake at our county fair. I had given her your recipe as it's our favorite cake. (Indiana) □This cake is a "seconds, please" dessert. Everyone loves it and asks for the recipe. We like it because it makes a generous cake and the icing is delicious. (Ohio) □I'm noted as a cake baker and Rocky Mountain Cake has helped me build my reputation. It's such an unusual cake and many who have tasted it have said they never had a cake quite like it. (Colorado)

ROCKY MOUNTAIN CAKE

2 c. sifted flour
1½ c. sugar
3 tsp. baking powder
1 tsp. salt
1 tsp. ground cinnamon
½ tsp. ground nutmeg
½ tsp. ground allspice
½ tsp. ground cloves
7 eggs, separated
2 tblsp. caraway seeds
½ c. cooking oil
¾ c. ice water
½ tsp. cream of tartar
Rocky Mountain Frosting (recipe
   follows)

Sift together flour, sugar, baking powder, salt, cinnamon, nutmeg, allspice and cloves.

Combine egg yolks, caraway seeds, oil and water in large bowl. Add dry ingredients. Beat at low speed with electric mixer 30 seconds.

Combine egg whites and cream of tartar in large bowl. Beat at high speed until stiff peaks form. Gently fold egg yolk mixture into egg whites. Turn batter into ungreased 10-inch tube pan.

Bake in 325° oven 55 minutes, then increase heat to 350° and bake 10 to 15 more minutes. Invert tube pan on funnel or bottle to cool. When completely cooled, remove from pan.

Prepare Rocky Mountain Frosting. Frost top and sides of cake. Makes 12 servings.

ROCKY MOUNTAIN FROSTING

½ c. butter or regular margarine
2½ tblsp. flour
¼ tsp. salt
½ c. milk
½ c. brown sugar, firmly packed
2 c. sifted confectioners sugar
1 tsp. vanilla
1 c. chopped black walnuts

Melt butter in saucepan. Blend in flour and salt. Cook over medium heat 1 minute (do not brown). Add milk; cook, stirring constantly, until thick. Add brown sugar; beat well with spoon. Add confectioners sugar; beat until thick and creamy. Add vanilla and walnuts. Or reserve walnuts and use to decorate cake.

Spicy Prune Cake is a delicious and easy summertime cake when there are picnics and family reunions. Every time I take it to a picnic I know I'll hear, "Who brought that cake?" That's my cue to find a pencil and paper and start writing the recipe. (Pennsylvania) □An excellent cake—I've served it at open house, wedding receptions, picnics, community dinners and holiday parties. Everyone who tastes this outstanding cake asks for the recipe—while reaching for a second helping. (Minnesota) □My sister makes and serves this cake in her restaurant. It's a popular cake with her customers. (Washington)

SPICY PRUNE CAKE

1 c. cooking oil
1½ c. sugar
3 eggs
2 c. sifted flour
1 tsp. baking powder
1 tsp. baking soda
½ tsp. salt
1 tsp. ground cinnamon
1 tsp. ground nutmeg
1 tsp. ground allspice
1 c. cooked, mashed prunes
1 c. buttermilk
1 c. chopped pecans
Caramel Glaze (recipe follows)

Beat together oil and sugar in bowl until well blended at medium speed of electric mixer. Add eggs, one at a time, beating well after each addition.

Sift together flour, baking powder, baking soda, salt, cinnamon, nutmeg and allspice. Add dry ingredients to creamed mixture alternately with prunes and buttermilk, beating well after each addition. Stir in pecans. Pour into greased and floured 13x9x2-inch baking pan.

Bake in 350° oven 35 minutes or until cake tests done.

Meanwhile, prepare Caramel Glaze during last 15

minutes of baking time. Place cake in pan on rack. Immediately pour hot Caramel Glaze over cake. Makes 16 servings.

CARAMEL GLAZE

1 c. sugar
½ c. buttermilk
½ tsp. baking soda
1 tblsp. light corn syrup
½ c. butter
½ tsp. vanilla

Combine sugar, buttermilk, baking soda, corn syrup, butter and vanilla in 2-qt. saucepan. Cook over low heat, stirring constantly, until mixture boils. Boil 10 minutes, stirring occasionally.

My husband's first dessert choice is a jelly roll. With Frozen Cake Roll, Four Ways, he has four choices in the freezer. Whenever he has a yen for a piece of jelly roll, it's ready and waiting. (Florida)   □This cake has become such a big seller at our church bake sales that I start taking orders three months ahead of the event. (North Carolina)   □My favorite company cake—it's delicious, elegant, make-ahead and a delight to serve. Always makes a big impression. (Colorado)   □A light and delicate cake. My children like this roll filled with home-made jam—it's always a special dessert because they picked the berries for the jam. (Pennsylvania)

FROZEN CAKE ROLL, FOUR WAYS

4 eggs
¾ c. sugar
1 tsp. vanilla
¾ c. sifted cake flour
¾ tsp. baking powder
¼ tsp. salt
Confectioners sugar
Strawberry Roll (recipe follows)
Pineapple Roll (recipe follows)
Butterscotch Roll (recipe follows)
Chocolate Roll (recipe follows)

Beat eggs, sugar and vanilla in bowl at high speed of electric mixer until light and lemon-colored.

Sift together cake flour, baking powder and salt. Add dry ingredients to egg mixture, mixing lightly with spoon. Spread batter in greased and brown paper-lined 15½x10½x1-inch jelly roll pan.

Bake in 375° oven 15 minutes or until cake tests done. Loosen cake from pan; invert onto clean towel which has been dusted with confectioners sugar. Trim dry edges. Roll cake up with towel. Cool well.

Unroll cake. Spread with filling. Reroll cake. Wrap and freeze seam side down. Recommended storage time: 1 month. (Unfilled cake rolls can be stored up to 6 months.)

To serve: Thaw cake roll. Spread top with glaze. Slice cake roll. Serve with sauce. Each roll makes 10 servings.

Note: For chocolate cake roll, follow basic cake recipe adding ¼ c. baking cocoa with flour.

STRAWBERRY ROLL

    1 c. heavy cream
    3 tblsp. sugar
    ¼ tsp. vanilla
    1 (10 oz.) pkg. frozen strawberries,
        thawed and drained
    1¼ c. strawberry jam
    1¼ c. light corn syrup

Whip cream in bowl with electric mixer until it begins to thicken. Gradually add sugar, beating until stiff peaks from. Fold in vanilla and strawberries. Fill cake roll. Combine strawberry jam and corn syrup in saucepan. Bring to a boil. Brush some of hot mixture on cake roll. Cool. Serve remaining strawberry sauce with cake roll.

PINEAPPLE ROLL

    1 c. heavy cream
    3 tblsp. sugar
    ¼ tsp. almond extract
    1 (8½ oz.) can crushed pineapple,
        drained
    ¼ c. apricot jam
    ¼ c. light corn syrup
    1 (8½ oz.) can crushed pineapple,
        drained
    1 c. light corn syrup

Whip cream with electric mixer until it begins to thicken. Gradually add sugar, beating until stiff peaks form. Fold in almond extract and 1 can pine-apple. Fill cake roll. Combine apricot jam and ¼ c. corn syrup in saucepan. Bring to a boil. Brush on top of cake roll.

Combine 1 can pineapple and 1 c. corn syrup in saucepan. Bring to a boil; cook until mixture thickens. Cool and serve Pineapple Sauce with cake roll.

BUTTERSCOTCH ROLL

1 c. heavy cream
3 tblsp. sugar
¼ tsp. vanilla
1 (3 oz.) can pecans, chopped
¼ c. light corn syrup
1 tblsp. melted butter or regular margarine
¼ c. chopped pecans
⅔ c. light corn syrup
1¼ c. brown sugar, firmly packed
¼ c. butter or regular margarine
¼ tsp. salt
1 (6 oz.) can evaporated milk

Whip cream in bowl with electric mixer until it begins to thicken. Gradually add sugar, beating until stiff peaks form. Fold in vanilla and 1 (3 oz.) can pecans. Fill cake roll. Combine ¼ c. corn syrup and 1 tblsp. butter in saucepan; heat well. Brush on top of cake roll. Sprinkle with ¼ c. pecans.

Combine ⅔ c. corn syrup, brown sugar, ¼ c. butter and salt in saucepan. Bring to a boil; cook until a thick heavy syrup is formed. Remove from heat; cool. Stir in evaporated milk. Serve Butterscotch Sauce with cake roll.

CHOCOLATE ROLL

1 c. heavy cream
3 tblsp. sugar
¼ tsp. vanilla
¼ c. confectioners sugar

**4 (1 oz.) squares unsweetened
  chocolate**
½ c. butter or regular margarine
**3 (6 oz.) cans evaporated milk
  (2¼ c.)**
3 c. sugar

Whip cream in bowl with electric mixer until it begins to thicken. Gradually add 3 tblsp. sugar, beating until stiff peaks form. Fold in vanilla. Fill cake roll. Sift confectioners sugar over top.

Combine chocolate, butter and evaporated milk in double boiler top. Heat over simmering water until butter and chocolate melt. Slowly add 3 c. sugar; cook until sugar dissolves. Remove from heat; cool. Refrigerate. Serve Chocolate Sauce with cake roll.

Frozen Cake Roll, Four Ways—recipe, page 208

Grand Champion Sponge Cake—recipe, page 214

Lemon Sunshine Cake—recipe, page 216

Lemon Cheese Cake—recipe, page 224

213

Your Grand Champion Sponge Cake won top honors for me at our county fair. The very best sponge cake I have ever made. (Indiana)   □I couldn't be without this recipe. During strawberry and peach season it's the base for homemade shortcake. It's my summer birthday gift along with a jar of homemade jam, and for family birthdays I split the cake into three layers, spread them with homemade jam and frost with whipped cream. (Connecticut)   □A light and flavorful cake—the pineapple frosting adds the perfect touch. So good to serve after a hearty meal. (South Dakota)   □My family always requests this cake for birthdays. We like it best made with turkey eggs. (California)

GRAND CHAMPION SPONGE CAKE

1¼ c. sifted flour
1 c. sugar
½ tsp. baking powder
½ tsp. salt
6 eggs, separated
1 tsp. cream of tartar
½ c. sugar
¼ c. water
1 tsp. vanilla
Pineapple Frosting (recipe follows)

Sift together flour, 1 c. sugar, baking powder and salt.

Beat egg whites in large bowl until frothy at high speed of electric mixer. Add cream of tartar. Gradually add ½ c. sugar, beating until stiff but not dry peaks form.

Combine egg yolks, water, vanilla and dry ingredients in mixing bowl. Beat at medium speed until thick and lemon-colored (about 4 minutes). Gradually fold egg yolk mixture into egg whites. Pour batter into ungreased 10-inch tube pan.

Bake in 350° oven 45 minutes or until cake tests done. Invert tube pan on funnel or bottle to cool. When completely cooled, remove from pan.

Prepare Pineapple Frosting. Frost sides and top of cake with frosting. Makes 12 servings.

PINEAPPLE FROSTING

¼ c. butter or regular margarine
¼ c. shortening
3 c. sifted confectioners sugar
1 (8½ oz.) can crushed pineapple, drained
⅛ tsp. salt
¼ tsp. vanilla
½ tsp. grated lemon rind

Cream together butter and shortening in small bowl at medium speed of electric mixer. Gradually add confectioners sugar, beating well until light and fluffy. Stir in pineapple, salt, vanilla and lemon rind; mix until blended.

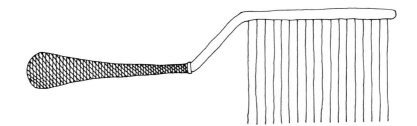

Lemon Sunshine Cake won a Grand Champion Award at our county fair. I'd been looking for an outstanding recipe for a cream-filled cake for years—finally discovered your Lemon Sunshine Cake. (Missouri) □ I have created many variations with your recipe for Lemon Sunshine Cake. For a birthday cake, I fill it with vanilla instant pudding, frost with a seven-minute frosting and lightly sprinkle with instant cocoa mix. Or, I cut cake in layers, spread generously with ice cream, and freeze for an hour. Dust with confectioners sugar and serve. My husband likes plain Sunshine Cake with a ladling of fresh fruit in season. (Wisconsin)

LEMON SUNSHINE CAKE

8 eggs, separated
½ c. sugar
2 tblsp. cold water
½ tsp. vanilla
½ tsp. almond extract
½ tsp. lemon extract
1¼ c. sifted flour
½ tsp. cream of tartar
½ tsp. salt
1 c. sugar
Lemon Custard Filling (recipe follows)
Confectioners sugar

Combine egg yolks, ½ c. sugar, water, vanilla, almond and lemon extracts in bowl. Beat at high speed of electric mixer until thick and lemon-colored (about 5 minutes). Stir in flour all at once.

Beat egg whites, cream of tartar and salt in large bowl at high speed until foamy. Gradually beat in 1 c. sugar, beating until stiff moist peaks form.

Gradually fold egg yolk mixture into egg whites. Pour into ungreased 10-inch tube pan. Pull spatula through batter once to break large air bubbles.

Bake in 325° oven 1 hour or until cake tests done. Invert tube pan on funnel or bottle to cool. When completely cooled, remove from pan.

Cut cake into 3 layers. Spread Lemon Custard Filling between layers. Dust top with confectioners sugar. Makes 12 servings.

LEMON CUSTARD FILLING

1 (2 oz.) envelope whipped topping
    mix
½ c. milk
1 tsp. vanilla
1 (3¼ oz.) pkg. instant lemon
    pudding mix
1 c. milk

Prepare whipped topping mix with ½ c. milk and vanilla according to package directions. Prepare pudding according to package directions, but using 1 c. milk. Fold pudding into topping mix.

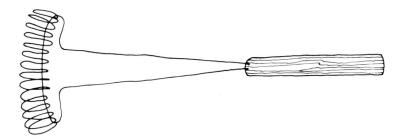

Your recipe for Yellow Lard Cake is one of the most popular cakes in our restaurant. The texture is excellent, it's moist, tender and, as our customers tell us, "a darn good cake." (Nebraska) □I bake for several customers for special occasions. Yellow Lard Cake makes a beautiful Wedding Cake as it stays moist and has such a delicate crumb. (Pennsylvania) □Do you know how hard it is to find good recipes for lard cakes? I finally found yours and have been making it ever since for family, potlucks, weddings and harvest crews. Always keep several in the freezer. (Oregon) □We render our own lard—it gives me such a feeling of pride and accomplishment when I use our lard to make this outstanding cake for my family. (Illinois)

YELLOW LARD CAKE

2 eggs, separated
½ c. sugar
2¼ c. sifted cake flour
1 c. sugar
3 tsp. baking powder
1 tsp. salt
⅓ c. lard
1 c. plus 2 tblsp. milk
1½ tsp. vanilla
Peanut Butter Frosting (recipe
  follows)
Basic Sugar Syrup (recipe follows)

Beat egg whites in small bowl until frothy at high speed of electric mixer. Gradually beat in ½ c. sugar, beating until very stiff glossy peaks are formed.

Sift together cake flour, 1 c. sugar, baking powder and salt.

Beat lard in mixing bowl until soft. Add dry ingredients, ¾ c. of the milk and vanilla. Beat at medium speed 1 minute. Scrape sides and bottom of bowl constantly. Add remaining milk and egg yolks. Beat at medium speed 1 minute, scraping bowl constantly. Fold in egg whites. Pour batter in 2 greased and floured 9-inch round cake pans.

Bake in 350° oven 25 to 30 minutes or until cakes test done. Cool in pans on racks 10 minutes. Remove from pans; cool on racks.

Prepare Peanut Butter Frosting. Fill and frost cake layers. Makes 12 servings.

PEANUT BUTTER FROSTING

¾ c. crunchy peanut butter
¾ c. Basic Sugar Syrup (recipe
   follows)

Whip peanut butter in bowl at medium speed of electric mixer. Gradually add Basic Sugar Syrup, beating well after each addition.

BASIC SUGAR SYRUP

2 c. sugar
1 c. water

Combine sugar and water in saucepan. Cook, stirring constantly, until mixture boils. Boil 1 minute. Remove from heat; pour into jar. Cool, cover and store in refrigerator. Makes about 2 cups.

Yellow Lard Cake—recipe, page 218

Gingerbread Deluxe—recipe, page 221

Gingerbread Deluxe is divine when it's served with a topping of homemade applesauce and whipped cream. (New Jersey) □A moist tender-crumbed gingerbread—my children's favorite lunchbox treat. (Montana) □I have three men to cook for and this recipe makes a good hearty dessert. For a special treat I top each serving with a scoop of orange sherbet. (Iowa)

GINGERBREAD DELUXE

2 c. sifted flour
2 tsp. baking powder
¾ tsp. salt
¼ tsp. baking soda
¾ tsp. ground ginger
¾ tsp. ground cinnamon
⅛ tsp. ground cloves
½ c. shortening
⅔ c. sugar
2 eggs
⅔ c. molasses
¾ c. boiling water
1 c. heavy cream, whipped and
    sweetened

Sift together flour, baking powder, salt, baking soda, ginger, cinnamon and cloves.

Cream together shortening and sugar in bowl until light and fluffy at medium speed of electric mixer. Add eggs, one at a time, beating well after each addition. Gradually beat in molasses.

Add dry ingredients, little by little, beating at low speed. Add water; beat until smooth. Pour batter into greased and floured 9-inch square baking pan.

Bake in 350° oven 35 to 45 minutes or until cake tests done. Cool in pan on rack until just warm. Serve topped with whipped cream. Makes 9 servings.

Black walnut trees are plentiful in our area—so are home-made black walnut cakes. This FARM JOURNAL recipe is superior. I bake it in a tube pan, frost with sea foam icing and sprinkle generously with coarsely chopped walnuts. Never even a tiny piece left when I take it to church suppers. (Oregon) □We like black walnuts—this is the best Black Walnut Cake recipe I have ever tried. I bake it every year for my husband's birthday and whenever I want a special company dessert. (Maryland)   □A week before Christmas my family knows that Mom will be baking their favorite Black Walnut Cake for Christmas Eve supper. (Tennessee)

BLACK WALNUT CAKE

3½ c. sifted cake flour
5 tsp. baking powder
1 tsp. salt
1¼ c. shortening
1½ c. sugar
1 tsp. almond extract
1 tsp. vanilla
4 eggs, separated
1½ c. milk
¼ c. sugar
1¼ c. chopped black walnuts
Chocolate Filling (recipe follows)
Sea Foam Frosting (recipe follows)

Sift together cake flour, baking powder and salt.

Cream together shortening and 1½ c. sugar in bowl until light and fluffy at medium speed of electric mixer. Add almond extract, vanilla and egg yolks; beat well. Add dry ingredients alternately with milk, beating well after each addition.

Beat egg whites in bowl at high speed until frothy. Gradually add ¼ c. sugar, beating until stiff glossy peaks are formed. Fold egg whites into batter. Fold in walnuts. Pour batter into 2 greased 9-inch round cake pans.

Bake in 350° oven 45 minutes or until cakes test done. Cool in pans on racks 10 minutes. Remove from pans; cool on racks.

Prepare Chocolate Filling. Cool well. Fill cake layers. Frost sides and top of cake with Sea Foam Frosting. Makes 12 servings.

CHOCOLATE FILLING

1 (3¼ oz.) pkg. chocolate pudding and
pie filling
1½ c. milk

Combine pudding mix and milk in saucepan. Cook over medium heat, stirring constantly, until mixture comes to a full bubbling boil. Remove from heat. Cool well.

SEA FOAM FROSTING

2 egg whites
1½ c. brown sugar, firmly packed
1 tblsp. light corn syrup
¼ c. water
¼ tsp. salt
1 tsp. vanilla

Combine egg whites, brown sugar, corn syrup, water and salt in top of double boiler; mix thoroughly. Cook over simmering water, beating constantly until peaks form (about 7 minutes). Remove from heat; add vanilla.

Beat until thick enough to spread.

Whenever I make Lemon Cheese Cake for my family, the time and effort it took to make this cake shows. It says, "I love you—you are important to me." (Tennessee) □Your recipe for Lemon Cheese Cake is the exact recipe my mother always baked for our Christmas cake—hunted for it for years. Fifteen years ago I found it in your cookbook, rushed into the kitchen and baked it—it looked and tasted just like Mother's! Now it is our Christmas cake and the recipe will be passed on to my daughter. (Iowa) □Our annual Farm Summer Picnic has been a tradition for 25 years. Every year there has been a Lemon Cheese Cake right in the center of the long picnic table. It's always the first dessert to disappear right down to the last crumb. (Pennsylvania)

LEMON CHEESE CAKE

1 c. butter or regular margarine
2 c. sugar
3 c. sifted cake flour
3 tsp. baking powder
¾ c. milk
6 egg whites
Lemon Cheese Cake Filling (recipe
    follows)

Cream together butter and sugar in bowl until light and fluffy.

Sift together cake flour and baking powder. Add dry ingredients alternately with milk, beating well after each addition.

Beat egg whites in bowl until stiff peaks form at high speed. Fold egg whites into creamed mixture. Pour batter into 3 greased and waxed paper-lined 8-inch round cake pans.

Bake in 350° oven 25 to 30 minutes or until cakes test done. Cool in pans on racks 10 minutes. Remove from pans; cool on racks.

Prepare Lemon Cheese Cake Filling. Fill layers. Frost sides and top of cake with your favorite seven-minute frosting, if you wish. Top can be decorated with coconut. Makes 12 servings.

LEMON CHEESE CAKE FILLING

½ c. butter or regular margarine
1 c. sugar
6 egg yolks
1 tblsp. grated lemon rind
⅓ c. lemon juice

Combine butter, sugar, egg yolks, lemon rind and lemon juice in top of double boiler. Place over simmering water. Cook, stirring constantly, until thick. Remove from heat; cool well.

Sour Cream Pound Cake is superb—plain, glazed or iced! (Missouri) ☐My husband tells me that it's a good down-to-earth cake—the kind he likes best. (California) ☐This pound cake never fails me. It turns out perfectly every time. It's truly an all-time favorite in our house. (New Jersey)

SOUR CREAM POUND CAKE

3 c. sifted flour
1 tsp. salt
¼ tsp. baking soda
1 c. butter
3 c. sugar
6 eggs
1 tsp. vanilla
1 tsp. almond extract
1 c. dairy sour cream
Confectioners sugar

Sift together flour, salt and baking soda.

Cream together butter and sugar in large bowl at medium speed of electric mixer until light and fluffy. Add eggs, one at a time, beating well after each addition. Add vanilla and almond extract. (Total beating time: 10 minutes.)

Add dry ingredients alternately with sour cream, beating well after each addition. Pour batter into well-greased 10-inch fluted tube pan.

Bake in 325° oven 1 hour or until cake tests done. Cool in pan on rack 10 minutes. Remove from pan. Cool on rack. Dust with confectioners sugar before serving. Makes 12 servings.

Boiled Raisin Cake reminds my husband and me of a cake our grandmothers baked in the old iron cook stove. (Maryland) □Our family likes a "fruity" cake that's plain, hearty and good—this cake is our standby. (Pennsylvania) □A wonderful moist, spicy cake that stays fresh for a long time—now there are only the two of us, and keeping quality is important. (Nevada) □Men head for this cake whenever I take it to a potluck. I substitute seeded muscats for the raisins and frost with an almond flavored icing. (Nebraska) □A good down-to-earth cake with just the right spiciness. (Minnesota)

BOILED RAISIN CAKE

1½ c. sugar
4 tblsp. baking cocoa
2½ c. water
⅔ c. butter or regular margarine
2 c. raisins
2 tsp. ground cinnamon
½ tsp. ground cloves
½ tsp. ground nutmeg
½ tsp. ground allspice
½ tsp. salt
3½ c. sifted flour
2 tsp. baking powder
1 tsp. baking soda
1 c. chopped walnuts

Mix together sugar and cocoa in 3-qt. saucepan. Add water, butter, raisins, cinnamon, cloves, nutmeg, allspice and salt; stir until blended. Bring to boiling; boil 4 minutes. Remove from heat; cool to room temperature.

Sift together flour, baking powder and baking soda. Add to raisin mixture, stirring with spoon until well blended. Stir in walnuts. Pour batter into greased 13x9x2-inch baking pan.

Bake in 350° oven 35 minutes or until cake tests done. Cool in pan on rack. Cut in squares. Makes 16 servings.

I collect lots of compliments whenever I serve your Cocoa Chiffon Cake. Even though I'm not a good cake baker, I always have wonderful results with this cake. (Nebraska) □We prefer this chocolate cake because it has a lighter chocolate flavor, not so rich and heavy as many cakes, and looks elegant. (California) □It's a beautiful showy cake—I make it for special occasions. (Kansas) □A versatile cake—can be served in so many ways for all kinds of occasions. (South Dakota)

COCOA CHIFFON CAKE

½ c. baking cocoa
¾ c. boiling water
1¾ c. sifted cake flour
1¾ c. sugar
1½ tsp. baking soda
1 tsp. salt
½ c. cooking oil
8 eggs, separated
2 tsp. vanilla
½ tsp. cream of tartar

Mix cocoa and boiling water; set aside.

Sift together cake flour, sugar, baking soda and salt into a large mixing bowl. Make a well in the center. Add oil, egg yolks, vanilla and cocoa mixture; beat well at medium speed of electric mixer (about 3 minutes).

Beat egg whites and cream of tartar at high speed until stiff peaks form. Fold egg whites into batter. Pour into ungreased 10-inch tube pan. Cut through batter with metal spatula to break large air bubbles.

Bake in 325° oven 55 minutes. Increase temperature to 350°; bake 10 minutes or until cake tests done. Invert cake to cool. When completely cooled, remove from pan. Makes 12 servings.

Champion Angel Food Cake was my first success after 15 years of trying to make a perfect angel food. (Maryland) □Such a tender cake and it is higher than many angel food cakes. Now it is the family birthday cake. (Nebraska) □I wish I'd discovered the recipe sooner in your book as I receive so many compliments whenever I serve your Champion Angel Food Cake. (Wisconsin) □We love this cake for two reasons. We raise chickens and have so many eggs—this cake is made often at our house. My husband must watch his cholesterol intake and he loves desserts. He beams when I serve this angel food cake with crushed fresh strawberries. (Iowa)

CHAMPION ANGEL FOOD CAKE

1¼ c. sifted cake flour
¾ c. sugar
1½ c. egg whites (10 to 11)
1½ tsp. cream of tartar
¼ tsp. salt
1 tsp. vanilla
1 c. sugar

Sift together cake flour and ¾ c. sugar twice.

Beat egg whites, cream of tartar, salt and vanilla in large mixing bowl until foamy at high speed of electric mixer. Add 1 c. sugar, 2 tblsp. at a time, beating until stiff glossy peaks form.

Add flour mixture in 4 parts, folding about 15 strokes after each addition. Spoon batter into ungreased 10-inch tube pan. Pull metal spatula through batter once to break large air bubbles.

Bake in 375° oven 35 to 40 minutes or until cake tests done. Invert tube pan on funnel or bottle to cool. When completely cooled, remove from pan. Makes 12 servings.

Chocolate Nut Loaf has been our family's chocolate cake for years. Your former editor Carroll Streeter visited us 35 years ago and we served him this cake—he pronounced it delicious. That's how it got into your cookbook! (Pennsylvania)   □It's quick and easy to put together and makes a hit with everyone. (Minnesota)   □This cake tastes good warm from the oven—needs no icing. I always bake several Chocolate Nut Loaves for my son to take back to college. (Ohio)   □Whenever my brother drops in for lunch, he asks me if we're going to have that good chocolate cake for dessert. (Wisconsin)

CHOCOLATE NUT LOAF

1 c. butter or regular margarine
2 c. sugar
5 eggs
2 (1 oz.) squares unsweetened
   chocolate, melted
1 tsp. vanilla
2½ c. sifted cake flour
1 tsp. baking soda
¼ tsp. salt
1 c. buttermilk
1 c. chopped walnuts

Cream together butter and sugar in bowl until light and fluffy at medium speed of electric mixer. Add eggs, one at a time, beating well after each addition. Add chocolate and vanilla; blend well.

Sift together cake flour, baking soda and salt. Add dry ingredients alternately with buttermilk, beating well after each addition. Stir in walnuts. Pour batter into 2 greased 8½x4½x2½-inch loaf pans.

Bake in 325° oven 1 hour or until cakes test done. Cool in pans on racks 10 minutes. Remove from pans; cool on racks. Loaves can be dusted with confectioners sugar before serving, if you wish. Makes 20 servings.

PIES
&
PIECRUSTS

PIES & PIECRUSTS

BUTTERSCOTCH MERINGUE PIE
BROWN-BUTTER BUTTERSCOTCH PIE
BEST-EVER LEMON MERINGUE PIE
RHUBARB-ORANGE CREAM PIE
SNOWSTORM SQUASH PIE
TAWNY PUMPKIN PIE
OLD-FASHIONED APPLE PIE
FROSTED BIG APPLE PIE
FRESH CHERRY PIE
VANILLA CREAM PIE
ELDERBERRY APPLE PIE
CHOCOLATE CHEESE PIE
PEANUT BUTTER PIE
STRAWBERRY GLACE PIE
DOUBLE-GOOD BLUEBERRY PIE
FRESH RHUBARB PIE
FLUFFY GRAPE PIE
USDA PECAN PIE
GLAZED STRAWBERRY-RHUBARB PIE
CHERRY PIE SPECIAL
COUNTRY TEAROOM PASTRY
EGG YOLK PASTRY

Pies that Please Everyone

Rather than try to make a decision on a single most-favorite recipe, some women who answered our letter expressed their enthusiasm for pie by voting for "the whole pie book."

That sums up the regard most American families have for pie. Of all the desserts in our many cookbooks, pies were most often voted top choice. Farm women have always been famous for their tender flaky pie crusts and great variety of delicious fillings. Most of the favorites in this chapter are men's choice—women give the highest ratings to pies that please their husbands!

With more than 700 recipes in the *Complete Pie Cookbook,* plus more pie recipes in our other cookbooks, choosing a favorite is not easy. So we must have been psychic back in the early sixties when we named a lemon pie Best-Ever Lemon Meringue Pie. That's what it turned out to be in this survey of 250,000 of our cookbook owners—the top pie for our *Farm Journal Best-Ever Recipes* cookbook!

Next was our Frosted Big Apple Pie, a two-crust pie big enough to serve 24, baked in a jelly roll pan. Fourth choice was another apple pie—Old-Fashioned Apple Pie with two variations—nosed out by Tawny Pumpkin Pie in third place.

Fruit pies reflect the bounty of orchard and garden—Double-Good Blueberry, Elderberry Apple Pie and Strawberry Glace. We've included three rhubarb pies that women told us were some of the best in the country: Rhubarb-Orange Cream Pie, Glazed Strawberry-Rhubarb and just plain but delicious Fresh Rhubarb Pie. And also Cherry Pie Special that won over 32 other cherry pies among the top favorites. Must be good!

Brown-Butter Butterscotch Pie and Butterscotch Meringue were heirloom recipes that many women remembered from their childhood, and after searching for over 30 years, trying out countless recipes in their kitchens, they finally found both recipes in a FARM JOURNAL cookbook. In fact, you may find one or two recipes as well as some heirlooms in all your favorite categories—even a fantastically smooth Chocolate Cheese Pie. The chapter ends with two very special pastry recipes.

After searching 32 years for a Butterscotch Meringue Pie like my husband's mother used to make, I found this recipe in your Country Cookbook. So I decided to try it. I was so happy to hear "That's it . . . that's the one!" Thanks to FARM JOURNAL. (Texas) □This is the first butterscotch pie recipe I have found that's easy to make and has old-fashioned richness. (Illinois) □Butterscotch is a favorite flavor of my family and I have never had a failure using this recipe. (Indiana)

BUTTERSCOTCH MERINGUE PIE

⅓ c. sifted flour
1 c. brown sugar, firmly packed
¼ tsp. salt
2 c. milk, scalded
3 egg yolks, slightly beaten
3 tblsp. butter or regular margarine
½ tsp. vanilla
1 baked 9-inch pie shell
3 egg whites
¼ tsp. salt
6 tblsp. sugar
½ tsp. vanilla

Combine flour, brown sugar and ¼ tsp. salt in 2-qt. saucepan. Gradually stir in milk. Cook over medium heat, stirring constantly, until mixture thickens and boils. Cook 2 minutes. Remove from heat.

Add small amount of hot mixture to egg yolks, then stir into remaining hot mixture. Cook 1 minute, stirring constantly. Remove from heat. Add butter and vanilla; cool slightly. Pour into pie shell.

Beat together egg whites and ¼ tsp. salt in bowl until frothy. Add sugar, 1 tblsp. at a time, beating until stiff glossy peaks form. Add ½ tsp. vanilla. Spread meringue over top of filling, sealing edges.

Bake in 350° oven 12 minutes or until meringue is golden brown. Cool on rack. Makes 6 to 8 servings.

Brown-Butter Butterscotch Pie is the best—really the best butterscotch pie I have ever made or tasted and I have a big collection of fine recipes . . . many handed-down heirlooms. It's my special pie for guests. (Indiana) □The flavor of this pie is superb. My husband requests this for his birthday and for Thanksgiving. I can never use packaged butterscotch pudding again. My family would protest—they've tasted the best. (Massachusetts) □ Your recipe is known in our community as Marilyn's Butterscotch Pie. At a pie fund-raising auction, my pie brought top money—51 dollars! (Indiana)

BROWN-BUTTER BUTTERSCOTCH PIE

6 tblsp. butter or regular margarine
1 c. dark brown sugar, firmly packed
1 c. boiling water
3 tblsp. cornstarch
2 tblsp. flour
½ tsp. salt
1⅔ c. milk
3 egg yolks, slightly beaten
1 tsp. vanilla
1 baked 9-inch pie shell
Sweetened whipped cream

Melt butter in heavy skillet over low heat. Watch carefully. When golden brown, add brown sugar. Cook, stirring constantly, until mixture comes to a boil. Stir in water and remove from heat.

Mix cornstarch, flour and salt in saucepan. Blend in milk, stirring until smooth. Stir in sugar mixture. Cook over medium heat, stirring constantly, until it comes to a boil. Boil 1 minute. Remove from heat.

Stir a little of hot mixture into egg yolks; then blend into hot mixture. Cook 1 minute. Remove from heat. Add vanilla. Cool slightly.

Pour into pie shell and chill. Top with whipped cream before serving. Makes 6 to 8 servings.

This pie is exactly what it is called—the best-ever lemon pie I have ever eaten. When our bridge club meets, the men come in asking, "Did you make your lemon pie for dessert?" (Ohio) □Most lemon pies are either too runny or too rubbery—your Best-Ever pie is perfect. It's light and delicate with just the right lemon tang. (California) □I've earned a reputation in my neighborhood as the most outstanding pie baker with this lemon pie recipe. (Illinois)

BEST-EVER LEMON MERINGUE PIE

1½ c. sugar
1½ c. water
½ tsp. salt
½ c. cornstarch
⅓ c. water
4 eggs, separated
½ c. lemon juice
3 tblsp. butter or regular margarine
1 tsp. grated lemon rind
¼ tsp. salt
½ c. sugar
1 baked 9-inch pie shell

Combine 1½ c. sugar, 1½ c. water and ½ tsp. salt in saucepan; heat to boiling. Mix cornstarch and ⅓ c. water to make smooth paste. Gradually add to boiling mixture, stirring constantly. Cook until thick and clear. Remove from heat.

Beat together egg yolks and lemon juice; stir into mixture. Return to heat. Cook, stirring constantly, until mixture bubbles again. Remove from heat. Stir in butter and lemon rind. Cover; cool to lukewarm.

Combine egg whites and ¼ tsp. salt in bowl; beat until frothy. Gradually add ½ c. sugar, beating until glossy peaks form. Stir 2 rounded tablespoonfuls of meringue into lukewarm filling. Pour into pie shell. Top with remaining meringue, spreading evenly.

Bake in 325° oven 15 minutes or until lightly browned. Makes 6 to 8 servings.

Best-Ever Lemon Meringue Pie—recipe, page 236

Even non-rhubarb eaters love Rhubarb-Orange Cream Pie! It's a never-fail recipe and makes use of all my surplus rhubarb. I freeze rhubarb so we can enjoy this pie in any season. (Washington)   □So different from any other rhubarb pie recipe I have used. My whole family likes it. (New York)   □The flavor is so distinctive and it uses ingredients I have on hand all the time. I serve it at special buffet supper functions. (Minnesota) □The pecans and orange juice complement the rhubarb flavor. A true company dessert but one we enjoy frequently during the season. (Pennsylvania)

RHUBARB-ORANGE CREAM PIE

3 eggs, separated
¼ c. sugar
¼ c. soft butter or regular margarine
3 tblsp. frozen orange juice
    concentrate
1 c. sugar
¼ c. flour
¼ tsp. salt
2½ c. rhubarb, cut in ½-inch pieces
1 unbaked 9-inch pie shell with fluted
    rim
⅓ c. chopped pecans

Beat egg whites in bowl until stiff. Gradually add ¼ c. sugar, beating well after each addition.

Add butter and orange concentrate to egg yolks; beat thoroughly. Add 1 c. sugar, flour and salt; beat well. Add rhubarb to yolk mixture; stir well. Gently fold in meringue. Pour into pastry-lined pan; sprinkle with pecans.

Bake on bottom rack in 375° oven 15 minutes. Reduce heat to 325°; bake 45 to 50 minutes more. Cool on rack. Makes 6 to 8 servings.

My college roommate always baked Snowstorm Squash Pie on cold wintry days. The apartment smelled like home as my mother has made this recipe for years. (California) □Sometimes I bake the filling in a casserole and serve it as a pudding with whipped cream and a dusting of cinnamon. (Illinois) □We raise many varieties of squash and each one has been used in this pie recipe many times. (Maine) □This combination of ingredients seems to bring out the wonderful flavor of squash; it has such a velvety custard texture. (New York)

SNOWSTORM SQUASH PIE

1¾ c. strained, mashed, cooked
  squash
1 c. sugar
1 tsp. salt
1 tsp. ground cinnamon
½ tsp. ground nutmeg
½ tsp. ground ginger
3 eggs
1½ c. milk
1 tblsp. butter or regular margarine
1 unbaked 9-inch pie shell

Combine squash, sugar, salt, cinnamon, nutmeg and ginger in bowl. Blend in eggs, milk and butter; mix well. Pour into pie shell.

Bake in 400° oven 50 minutes or until knife inserted in filling 1-inch from pie's edge comes out clean. Cool on rack. Serve slightly warm or cold. Makes 6 to 8 servings.

Even though I'm a good pie baker, pumpkin pie never turned out to suit me until I made Tawny Pumpkin Pie. Never have a soggy crust with this recipe and I have lots of praise from family and relatives when I serve it for Thanksgiving Dinner. (Minnesota) □This pie always turns out just right. The spices never rise to the surface and it's seasoned perfectly. When I asked my five-year-old son what kind of cake I should bake for his Dad's birthday, he suggested pumpkin pie. (Illinois) □Many people who don't like pumpkin pie ask for seconds when they sample this one. One of our guests who said he disliked pumpkin pie decided to try a small piece. He ended up eating half a pie! (Texas)

TAWNY PUMPKIN PIE

1¼ c. cooked mashed or canned
 pumpkin
¾ c. sugar
½ tsp. salt
1 tsp. ground cinnamon
¼ tsp. ground ginger
1 tsp. flour
2 eggs, slightly beaten
1 c. evaporated milk
2 tblsp. water
½ tsp. vanilla
1 unbaked 9-inch pie shell

Combine pumpkin, sugar, salt, spices and flour in mixing bowl. Add eggs; mix well. Add evaporated milk, water and vanilla; mix. Pour into pie shell.

Bake in 400° oven 45 to 50 minutes or until knife inserted near center comes out clean. Cool on rack. Makes 6 to 8 servings.

My family selected Old-Fashioned Apple Pie as their favorite apple pie. (Ohio)   □This pie uses inexpensive ingredients always found in my cupboard. I make it often and get many compliments. (Indiana)   □I especially like this pie made with green apples. The pie turns out plump and juicy. (North Dakota) □This recipe is so typical of FARM JOURNAL cookbooks . . . dependable, explicit and chatty. I use this recipe when the MacIntosh are ripe in our orchard and treat my children to warm pie before they start the evening chores. (Wisconsin)

OLD-FASHIONED APPLE PIE

¾ to 1 c. sugar
2 tblsp. flour
½ to 1 tsp. ground cinnamon
⅛ tsp. ground nutmeg
¼ tsp. salt
6 to 7 c. sliced pared apples
   (¼-inch slices)
Pastry for 2-crust 9-inch pie
2 tblsp. butter or regular margarine

Combine sugar, flour, cinnamon, nutmeg and salt in bowl. Add apples; mix lightly. Heap in pastry-lined 9-inch pie pan. Dot with butter. Adjust top crust and flute edges; cut vents.

Bake in 425° oven 50 to 60 minutes or until crust is browned and apples are tender. Cool on rack. Makes 6 to 8 servings.

Dutch-Style Apple Pie: Cut large vents in top crust and omit butter. Five minutes before baking time is up, remove pie from oven and pour ½ c. heavy cream into pie through vents. Return to oven and complete baking.

Cinnamon Apple Pie: Omit cinnamon and nutmeg and add 3 tblsp. red cinnamon candies (red hots) to sugar. Use a lattice past top if desired.

Frosted Big Apple Pie made with tart Jonathan apples and spices produces a pie that's heavenly eating. (Kansas) □A big fast-fix apple pie that will serve 24 people. (California) □Every time I make this apple pie, half is gone before the pie is cooled. My family likes it very warm with a big pour of heavy cream. (Wisconsin) □A perfect pie to serve hungry ranchers. I have taken this 40 miles up the mountains when we are branding calves. The pie freezes well so it can be made ahead of the busy season. (Maryland)

FROSTED BIG APPLE PIE

Egg yolk pastry (see Index)
4 tsp. lemon juice
5 lbs. pared tart apples, thinly sliced
    (12 to 15 c.)
¾ c. sugar
¾ c. brown sugar, firmly packed
1 tsp. ground cinnamon
½ tsp. ground nutmeg
¼ tsp. salt
Milk
Sugar

Roll out half of Egg Yolk Pastry into rectangle large enough to fit 15½x10½x1-inch jelly roll pan. Sprinkle lemon juice on apples. Place half of apples in pastry-lined pan.

Combine ¾ c. sugar, brown sugar, cinnamon, nutmeg and salt in bowl; mix well. Sprinkle half of mixture over apples. Spread remaining apples on top and sprinkle with remaining sugar mixture.

Roll out remaining pastry to fit top. Seal and crimp edges. Brush with milk and sprinkle with sugar. Cut vents in top crust.

Bake in 400° oven 50 minutes or until crust is golden brown and apples are tender. Cool in pan on rack. When cool, drizzle with your favorite confectioners sugar icing. Makes 24 servings.

We have cherry trees and freeze cherries each spring so I can make Fresh Cherry Pie all year round. I always reserve some frozen cherries for my husband's birthday in October. I bake him three special cherry pies on that day—to serve all his friends. (Missouri) □This pie has become our traditional Fourth of July pie. For a patriotic red, white and blue effect, I top each wedge of pie with vanilla ice cream and garnish with fresh blue mulberries. (Nebraska) □A much used and valued addition to my recipe file. My mom was a cake baker so I didn't have any pie recipes from her. Now this recipe has become my husband's favorite . . . I am so proud. (Illinois)

FRESH CHERRY PIE

1⅓ c. sugar
⅓ c. flour
⅛ tsp. salt
3 drops almond extract
4 c. pitted tart cherries
Pastry for 2-crust 9-inch pie
2 tblsp. butter or regular margarine

Combine sugar, flour and salt in bowl. Add almond extract and cherries. Toss with sugar-flour mixture, mixing thoroughly.

Roll out half of pastry. Fit in 9-inch pie plate. Turn cherry mixture into pastry-lined pie plate. Dot with butter. Roll out remaining pastry; cut in ½-inch strips. Arrange on top of pie in lattice pattern; flute edges.

Bake in 425° oven 40 minutes or until crust is golden brown. If edges brown too much, cover with strip of aluminum foil. Cool on rack. Makes 6 to 8 servings.

Note: Use 1½ c. sugar if you like a sweeter pie.

Fresh Cherry Pie—recipe, page 243

244

Vanilla Cream Pie—recipe, page 246

I couldn't begin to count the compliments I have received on your recipe for Vanilla Cream Pie. I also use it as the base for my coconut and banana cream pies. It's simpler to make than most and always turns out smooth and creamy. (New York) □I make the filling and forget the pie shell as my husband thinks this is the world's greatest pudding topped with canned sour cherries. (South Dakota) □This recipe never fails me. I can create so many variations from one recipe. (Ohio) □An easy, economical pie that fits into family dinners, church suppers or for any occasion I need to make a pie that I know I will be proud to serve. (Indiana) □Every year we have a Turkey Supper at church to raise money. The traditional dessert is your Vanilla Cream Pie. (Nebraska)

VANILLA CREAM PIE

½ c. sugar
3 tblsp. flour
1 tblsp. cornstarch
¼ tsp. salt
1½ c. milk
3 egg yolks, slightly beaten
1 tblsp. butter or regular margarine
1 tsp. vanilla
1 baked 8-inch pie shell

Combine sugar, flour, cornstarch and salt in top of double boiler. Gradually blend in milk, then add egg yolks and butter.

Place over rapidly boiling water so pan is touching water. Cook, stirring constantly, until thick and smooth, about 7 minutes. Remove from heat. Add vanilla. Stir until smooth and blended. Pour hot filling into pie shell. Chill several hours before serving. Makes 6 to 8 servings.

Chocolate Cream Pie: Melt 1½ squares unsweetened chocolate in milk in top of double boiler. Set aside to cool. Then proceed as directed for Vanilla Cream Pie, using the chocolate-milk mixture and increasing sugar from ½ to ¾ c.

Strawberry Sponge Cream Pie: Drain 1 (10 oz.) pkg. partially thawed frozen strawberries, reserving juice. If necessary, add water to make ½ c. juice. Combine 2 tblsp. cornstarch and 1 tblsp. sugar in small saucepan; slowly add juice, stirring to make smooth paste. Cook over low heat, stirring constantly, until mixture is thick and clear. Remove from heat and stir in strawberries. Set aside. Prepare filling for Vanilla Cream Pie, reducing flour to 2 tblsp. and egg yolks to 2. Pour into baked 9-inch pie shell. Beat egg whites at high speed until frothy. Gradually add 3 tblsp. sugar, beating at high speed until very stiff peaks form. Fold thickened fruit into egg whites. Spread evenly on hot cream filling, sealing to crust all around. Bake in 350° oven about 30 minutes. Cool before serving.

Raspberry Cream Pie: Follow directions for Strawberry Sponge Cream Pie, substituting raspberries for strawberries.

Blueberry Cream Pie: Follow directions for Strawberry Sponge Cream Pie, substituting blueberries for strawberries. Add 1 tsp. lemon juice.

Cherry Cream Pie: Add 2 tsp. unflavored gelatin to dry ingredients and cook filling as directed for Vanilla Cream Pie. Cover and set aside. Add ¼ tsp. salt to 3 egg whites; beat until frothy. Gradually add 3 tblsp. sugar, beating until stiff peaks form. Beat half of meringue into cream filling until mixture is smooth. Fold remaining meringue into mixture. Spread 1 c. canned or homemade cherry pie filling on bottom of baked 9-inch pie shell. Cover with cream filling. Chill several hours before serving.

Butterscotch Cream Pie: Substitute ¾ c. brown sugar for sugar and increase butter to 2 tblsp. Proceed as directed for Vanilla Cream Pie.

Black Bottom Pie: Add 2 tsp. unflavored gelatin to dry ingredients. Cook filling as directed in recipe for Vanilla Cream Pie. Add ½ c. hot filling to ½ c. semisweet chocolate pieces, stir until they melt and mixture is smooth. Spread chocolate mixture in bottom of baked 9-inch pie shell. Cover and set remaining filling aside. Add ¼ tsp. salt to 3 egg whites; beat until frothy. Gradually add 3 tblsp. sugar, beating until stiff peaks form. With beater, beat half of this meringue into cream filling until mixture is smooth. Fold remaining half of meringue into mixture. Spread on chocolate layer in pie shell. Chill pie several hours before serving.

My husband and sons volunteer gladly to pick and clean elderberries so they can have Elderberry Apple Pie. I freeze about 20 pints of elderberries so I can have plenty on hand to make pies for Thanksgiving and fall card parties. (Ohio) □Elderberries grow wild in our area so this is an inexpensive as well as delicious pie to make. (Illinois) □We look forward to the hunting season every year. We may not come home with any game but we know we will come home with plenty of big juicy elderberries. And my husband knows as soon as we get home, I'll make several of his favorite Elderberry Apple Pies. (Oregon) □A thrifty, tasty pie that everyone thinks is so unusual—I call it my conversation pie. (Pennsylvania)

ELDERBERRY APPLE PIE

2 c. elderberries
1½ c. chopped pared tart apples
1 c. sugar
⅛ tsp. salt
3 tblsp. quick-cooking tapioca
Pastry for 2-crust 9-inch pie
2 tblsp. butter or regular margarine

Wash and stem elderberries.

Combine elderberries, apples, sugar, salt and tapioca in bowl, crushing berries with spoon.

Roll out half of pastry. Line 9-inch pie plate with pastry.

Spoon mixture into pie shell; dot with butter. Roll out remaining pastry and cut in ½-inch strips. Arrange on top of pie, making lattice top.

Bake in 400° oven 35 to 40 minutes or until apples are tender and crust is golden. Cool on rack. Makes 6 to 8 servings.

Chocolate Cheese Pie is definitely a company dessert, rich and delicious. It appeals to all cheesecake fanciers. (New Jersey) □A pie that never fails to bring raves. I sometimes freeze it and serve as an ice cream type dessert. (Wyoming) □A favorite pie with me as it's easy to fix, uses everyday ingredients that I have on hand and can be made a day ahead of a big dinner party. (New Hampshire) □Such a different pie with an unusual chocolate crust—a double treat for chocolate lovers. I always make it for birthdays, holidays and very special occasions. (North Carolina) □My husband suggests that I make this pie whenever we have company. (Michigan)

CHOCOLATE CHEESE PIE

Chocolate Graham Crust (recipe
   follows)
1 (6 oz.) pkg. semisweet chocolate
   pieces
1 (8 oz.) pkg. cream cheese, softened
½ c. light brown sugar, firmly packed
⅛ tsp. salt
1 tsp. vanilla
2 eggs, separated
¼ c. light brown sugar, firmly packed
1 cup heavy cream , whipped

Prepare Chocolate Graham Crust.

Melt chocolate over hot (not boiling) water; cool about 10 minutes.

Blend cream cheese, ½ c. brown sugar, salt and vanilla in bowl. Beat in egg yolks, one at a time. Beat in cooled chocolate; blend well.

Beat egg whites in bowl until stiff but not dry. Gradually beat in ¼ c. brown sugar; beat until stiff and glossy. Fold chocolate mixture into beaten whites. Fold in whipped cream.

Pour into chilled crust, reserving ¼ of mixture for decorating. Chill until filling sets slightly. Drop reserved mixture in mounds over top of pie. Chill overnight. Makes 8 servings.

CHOCOLATE GRAHAM CRUST

1½ c. graham cracker crumbs
¼ c. brown sugar, firmly packed
⅛ tsp. ground nutmeg
⅓ c. melted butter or regular
    margarine
1 (1 oz.) square unsweetened
    chocolate, melted

Combine graham cracker crumbs, brown sugar and nutmeg in bowl. Add butter and chocolate; mix thoroughly. Press mixture into 9-inch pie plate. Chill until firm.

Chocolate Cheese Pie—recipe, page 250

Peanut Butter Pie—recipe, page 253

At least once a month my teen-agers head for the kitchen and whip up a Peanut Butter Pie to surprise their Dad. (Iowa) □Such a different and delicious pie—great to serve for dessert after a heavy meal. (New York)   □My family loves peanut butter—they tell me that Peanut Butter Pie is the most super dessert in the world. We use chunk-style for extra crunch. (Oregon)   □Each member of our luncheon group was asked to make a new recipe and then take it to the club. I tried your recipe for Peanut Butter Pie—it was the hit of the afternoon. Now it's in my ''favorite pies'' file. (Michigan)

PEANUT BUTTER PIE

1 env. unflavored gelatin
¼ c. cold water
3 egg yolks, well beaten
¼ c. sugar
½ tsp. salt
¼ c. water
½ c. smooth peanut butter
½ c. water
½ tsp. vanilla
3 egg whites
¼ c. sugar
1 baked 9-inch pie shell

Soften gelatin in ¼ c. cold water. Combine egg yolks, ¼ c. sugar, salt and ¼ c. water in top of double boiler; blend. Stir in gelatin mixture. Place over boiling water. Beat constantly with rotary beater until thick and fluffy (about 5 minutes). Remove from heat; cool well.

Place peanut butter in bowl. Slowly beat in ½ c. water. Blend egg yolk mixture into peanut butter; add vanilla. Chill until slightly thickened, but still syrupy (10 to 15 minutes).

Beat egg whites until foamy. Gradually add ¼ c. sugar, beating until stiff. Fold into peanut butter mixture. Turn into pie shell. Chill until set.

Top with whipped cream and decorate with daisies made of peanut halves with chocolate pieces in center if you wish. Makes 6 to 8 servings.

If your family likes strawberries, you had better make two Strawberry Glace Pies—one doesn't last long. (Missouri) □A must during the strawberry season—tastes so fresh. I receive compliments galore every time I make it. (Louisiana) □Delicious and unusual. Makes a very special dessert for entertaining—easy on the hostess. (Delaware) □This pie looks so pretty on a buffet table. Tastes like spring. (Utah) □There's nothing that can compete with the fresh taste of strawberries, and this pie does capture the fresh taste. My husband tells me it's the best strawberry pie he has ever eaten. (Kansas) □My family likes this pie because it isn't too sweet, and the fresh natural taste of the berries comes through. (New York)

STRAWBERRY GLACE PIE

1½ qts. strawberries
1 c. sugar
3 tblsp. cornstarch
½ c. water
1 tblsp. butter or regular margarine
1 baked 9-inch pie shell
1 c. heavy cream
2 tblsp. confectioners sugar

Hull and wash strawberries; drain well. Crush enough (with potato masher) to make 1 c.

Combine sugar and cornstarch in saucepan. Add crushed berries and water. Cook over medium heat, stirring constantly, until mixture comes to a boil. Continue cooking and stirring over low heat 2 minutes. The mixture will be thickened and translucent. Remove from heat and stir in butter. Cool.

Place whole berries in pie shell, reserving a few choice ones for garnishing. Pour cooked mixture over berries. Cover and chill at least 2 hours.

Whip cream in bowl with electric mixer until it begins to thicken. Gradually add confectioners sugar, beating until soft peaks form. Garnish pie with whipped cream and additional whole strawberries. Makes 6 to 8 servings.

We love Double-Good Blueberry Pie—it's like eating fresh berries in a pie crust. (Illinois)   □The texture of the whole un-cooked berries in this makes it extra-special. When I want to make my family very happy, I bake this pie. (Maine)   □We love this pie. I've used it with other fruits, too. I substitute tapioca for the cornstarch. (Ohio)   □We raise blueberries and I'm always looking for new and different ways to serve them. The combi-nation of fresh and cooked berries in this pie gives it a unique taste. (Oregon)   □I shared this pie recipe with a neighbor. Her daughter won a blue ribbon when she entered the pie at the fair. (Michigan)   □A simple but elegant pie. We like the good berry taste. (New Hampshire)

DOUBLE-GOOD BLUEBERRY PIE

¾ c. sugar
3 tblsp. cornstarch
⅛ tsp. salt
¼ c. water
2 c. blueberries
1 tblsp. butter or regular margarine
1 tblsp. lemon juice
2 c. blueberries
1 baked 9-inch pie shell
Sweetened whipped cream

Combine sugar, cornstarch and salt in saucepan. Add water and 2 c. blueberries. Cook over medium heat, stirring constantly, until mixture comes to a boil and is thickened and clear. (Mixture will be quite thick.)

Remove from heat, and stir in butter and lemon juice. Cool.

Place remaining 2 c. blueberries in pie shell. Top with cooked blueberry mixture. Chill. Serve gar-nished with sweetened whipped cream. Makes 6 to 8 servings.

My sister and I team up and spend a whole day making and freezing Fresh Rhubarb Pie. (Indiana) □This rhubarb pie is the greatest—think it's the little touch of orange rind that makes it so good. (Iowa) □We like the tangy orange flavor. Just fabulous tasting—outdoes all other rhubarb pies. (Iowa) □The best rhubarb pie ever and the only rhubarb pie that my family likes. If I don't have orange rind on hand, I substitute three tablespoons of concentrated frozen orange juice. (New York) □I've made this for church and club gatherings for years. Everyone tells me it's the best of the rhubarb pie recipes in the county. (Illinois)

FRESH RHUBARB PIE

1⅓ c. sugar
⅓ c. flour
½ tsp. grated orange rind
⅛ tsp. salt
4 c. (½-inch pieces) fresh rhubarb
Pastry for 2-crust 9-inch pie
2 tblsp. butter or regular margarine

Combine sugar, flour, orange rind and salt in bowl. Add rhubarb; mix well.

Roll out half of pastry. Fit into 9-inch pie plate. Add rhubarb filling; dot with butter. Roll out remaining pastry for top crust.

Adjust top crust and flute edges to make high rim. Cut vents.

Bake in 425° oven 40 to 50 minutes or until juice begins to bubble through vents and crust is golden brown. Cool on rack. Pie is delicious served slightly warm. Makes 6 to 8 servings.

Spiced Rhubarb Pie: Omit the grated orange rind and add ¼ tsp. ground nutmeg.

Pineapple-Rhubarb Pie: Substitute 1 (8½ oz.) can crushed pineapple, drained, for 1 c. rhubarb.

Fluffy Grape Pie is such a light, tangy dessert after a hearty meal. (Maryland) □Such a different pie—many friends guess it's raspberry-flavored and are surprised to discover it's grape. During the Concord grape season, I freeze at least 20 one-cup units of puree. The green Concords work just as well. For a change I make a graham cracker crust instead of the pastry. (New Mexico) □I always receive lots of compliments when I serve this Grape Pie—guests think it's so unique. (Connecticut) □I make homemade grape juice, so I always have lots of puree to make this pie. My family always looks forward to the grape harvest as they know they'll be treated to their special pie. (Missouri)

FLUFFY GRAPE PIE

1 lb. fresh Concord grapes
¼ c. water
1 (3 oz.) pkg. lemon flavor gelatin
¾ c. sugar
1½ c. heavy cream, whipped
1 baked 9-inch pie shell

Wash and stem grapes. Heat grapes in Dutch oven over low heat 8 to 10 minutes to loosen skins. Do not boil. Remove from heat. Put grapes through food mill or wide-mesh strainer. Discard skins and seeds. (You will need 1 c. puree.)

Combine grape puree and water in saucepan. Bring to a boil. Remove from heat. Add lemon gelatin and stir until dissolved. Add sugar; mix well. Put into bowl; cover. Chill until mixture mounds when dropped from spoon, stirring occasionally.

Beat mixture until fluffy. Fold in whipped cream. Pour into pie shell. Refrigerate at least 2 hours or overnight. Serve topped with whipped cream if you wish. Makes 6 to 8 servings.

Note: Puree can be frozen ahead. You will need approximately 1 lb. fresh Concord grapes for each cup of puree.

I have used this USDA Pecan Pie recipe so often that my Pie Cookbook falls open to the page. (Texas) □The most elegant pecan pie recipe I have ever made. I have a standing order for two of these pies for our annual Ladies' Club Picnic. (Wisconsin) □My husband tells me to forget every other kind of pie during the holidays—just make lots of pecan pies. (Massachusetts) □This recipe makes a generous 10-inch pie—so many recipes make smaller skimpier pies. (Iowa) □Last year I turned out 17 of these rich pecan pies for Christmas. I substitute slivered almonds for pecans for a change. (Oklahoma)

USDA PECAN PIE

4 eggs
1 c. sugar
⅛ tsp. salt
1½ c. dark corn syrup
2 tblsp. plus 1 tsp. melted butter
1 tsp. vanilla
1 c. pecan halves
1 unbaked 10-inch pie shell

Preheat oven to 350°.

Beat eggs in bowl with rotary beater just until blended, but not frothy. Add sugar, salt and corn syrup. Add melted butter and vanilla, mixing just enough to blend. Spread pecans in bottom of pie shell. Pour in filling. Place pie in oven.

Reduce heat to 325° at once. Bake 50 to 60 minutes or until crust is golden brown and custard is set. Cool on rack. Makes 8 to 10 servings.

My husband's birthday pie was always rhubarb until he tasted Glazed Strawberry-Rhubarb Pie—now that is His Pie. I reduce the sugar to one cup as we like a tart pie. (Florida) ☐Strawberries are a family favorite and we always have an abundance of rhubarb—this pie combines the two deliciously. (Iowa)   ☐My nephew comes to visit every spring. The very first day he asks if I plan to make that rhubarb-strawberry pie—of course I've already made one for a dinner surprise. (Michigan) ☐We grow our own rhubarb and strawberries so this is a popular pie and very festive to look at, too. (Indiana)

GLAZED STRAWBERRY-RHUBARB PIE

1¼ c. sugar
⅛ tsp. salt
⅓ c. flour
Pastry for 2-crust 9-inch pie
2 c. fresh strawberries
2 c. (1-inch pieces) fresh rhubarb
2 tblsp. butter or regular margarine
1 tblsp. sugar

Combine 1¼ c. sugar, salt and flour in bowl; mix well. Roll out half of pastry. Fit into 9-inch pie plate.

Arrange half of strawberries and rhubarb in pastry-lined pie plate. Sprinkle with half of sugar mixture.

Repeat with remaining fruit and sugar mixture; dot with butter.

Roll out remaining pastry. Adjust top crust and flute edges. Brush top of pie with cold water and sprinkle on 1 tblsp. sugar. Cut vents in top.

Bake in 425° oven 40 to 50 minutes or until rhubarb is tender and crust is browned. Cool on rack. Makes 6 to 8 servings.

Note: You can top with a lattice instead of regular top crust, if you wish.

This has to be the best cherry pie anyone has ever eaten. It turns out picture-perfect every time. (Virginia)   □My daughter has made Cherry Pie Special for so many 4-H demonstrations. (Maryland)   □I adapt this recipe for frozen, canned and fresh cherries. We eat this year round—always with a big scoop of vanilla ice cream. (Massachusetts)   □The very first time I made Cherry Pie Special I made 11 pies for our annual club luncheon. Every one was a beauty. (Wyoming)

CHERRY PIE SPECIAL

2 (1 lb.) cans pitted tart red cherries
1 c. sugar
2½ tblsp. quick-cooking tapioca
¼ tsp. salt
¼ tsp. almond extract
1 tsp. lemon juice
4 drops red food color
Pastry for 2-crust 9-inch pie
1 tblsp. butter or regular margarine
¼ c. sugar
Sugar

Drain cherries, reserving ⅓ c. liquid. Combine 1 c. sugar, tapioca, salt, almond extract, lemon juice, red food color and reserved ⅓ c. liquid in bowl; mix well. Add cherries; let stand 15 minutes.

Arrange cherry mixture in pastry-lined pie plate. Dot with butter. Sprinkle with ¼ c. sugar. Roll out remaining pastry and cut in strips. Top filling with strips arranged in lattice fashion. Sprinkle top of pie with sugar. Cover pie rim with strip of aluminum foil.

Bake in 425° oven 40 minutes or until golden brown. Cool on rack. Makes 6 to 8 servings.

I've never had a tough crust since I started making Country Tearoom Pastry. I freeze several pie shells ahead for a busy day when I can't make pie crust from scratch. (Minnesota) □So light and flaky—I use it to make pie crust cookies. Roll the dough thin and sprinkle it with sugar and cinnamon. Then cut in small squares. Such a special treat! (Michigan) □I like Country Tearoom Pastry because it's so easy and it never fails. (Indiana) □'Tis a marvelous flaky pastry—just about the best I've ever tried. I always use this pastry for special occasions and holidays because it is so rich. (Connecticut)

COUNTRY TEAROOM PASTRY

4 c. sifted flour
1 tblsp. sugar
1½ tsp. salt
1½ c. lard
1 egg
1 tblsp. vinegar
½ c. cold water

Sift together flour, sugar and salt in bowl. Cut in lard with pastry blender or two knives until particles are the size of peas.

Beat egg in bowl. Blend in vinegar and water. Sprinkle over flour mixture, a tablespoon at a time, tossing with fork to mix. Gather dough together with fingers so it cleans the bowl. Chill before rolling. Makes enough pastry for two 2-crust 9-inch pies and one 9-inch pie shell.

It would be hard to choose my family's favorite pie because they like pie, period. However, I know which pastry they like best. . . Egg Yolk Pastry. I always have crust frozen in the freezer. (Oklahoma) □This recipe is dependable, light and flaky. I'm always asked to bring pies to covered dish dinners since I started to use this recipe. (Michigan) □When my married daughter asked for help in making pastry, I naturally gave her my recipe for Egg Yolk Pastry. She doesn't have trouble making excellent piecrusts now. (Wisconsin)

EGG YOLK PASTRY

5 c. sifted flour
4 tsp. sugar
½ tsp. salt
½ tsp. baking powder
1½ c. lard
2 egg yolks
Cold water

Sift together flour, sugar, salt and baking powder into bowl. Cut in lard with pastry blender until coarse crumbs form. Beat egg yolks in measuring cup. Add enough cold water to make a scant cupful.

Gradually add egg yolk mixture to crumb mixture, tossing lightly with fork until dough begins to hold together. Form into a ball. Divide dough in sixths. Roll out one sixth of dough on lightly floured surface to ⅛-inch thickness. Fit into pie plate, using care not to stretch dough. Trim even with edge of pie plate. Fill with desired filling.

Roll second sixth of dough to ⅛-inch thickness. Place over filling. Trim to within ½-inch from the edge of pie plate. Fold top edge under bottom crust and press to seal. Make a rim; flute edge.

Cut vents in top crust to allow steam to escape. Bake as pie recipe directs. Repeat with remaining dough. Makes enough pastry for three 2-crust 9-inch pies or Frosted Big Apple Pie (see Index).

COOKIES

COOKIES

FUDGE NUT BARS
BROWNIES FOR A CROWD
PUMPKIN PIE SQUARES
LEMON-COCONUT SQUARES
CORN FLAKE COOKIES
OATMEAL/COCONUT CRISPS
OATMEAL CHIPPERS
BEST-EVER BUTTERSCOTCH COOKIES
OATMEAL/MOLASSES COOKIES
ORANGE/COCONUT CRISPS
BROWNIES
LEMON LOVE NOTES
SAUCEPAN BROWNIES
CRACKLE-TOP GINGER COOKIES
OATMEAL/CHOCOLATE BARS
CHOCOLATE MACAROONS
GRANDMA'S SOFT SUGAR COOKIES
DANISH APPLE BARS

Candidates for the Cookie Jar

If everyone in your house prefers brownies over all other cookies that you bake, they are in complete agreement with the women who named their favorite FARM JOURNAL recipes. Three out of 40 of the brownie recipes in our cookbooks totaled the most votes in the cookie category, and Brownies for a Crowd got more than half the brownie votes—proving families not only like brownies, they like lots of them!

The second favorite cookie may surprise you—unless, of course, you've made them yourself. Then Pumpkin Pie Squares will be no surprise. This unusual cookie, which you eat with a fork, was one of several Pie-Bar cookies developed especially for FARM JOURNAL'S *Homemade Cookies* book in 1971. This recipe gives dieters a choice between denying themselves pie for dessert and having just a bite of delicious sweetness to top off a meal. The recipe for Danish Apple Bars from our *Country Fair Cookbook* is another pie-type cookie that ranked among the first five.

Three oatmeal cookies turned up among the favorites: Oatmeal/Coconut Crisps—a huge recipe that makes 14 dozen cookies—Oatmeal/Molasses Cookies and Oatmeal Chippers (made with chocolate chips, of course).

As you read comments accompanying other recipe choices in this chapter, you'll see that cookie recipes become favorites for all kinds of reasons: Because they're quick to make. Because the recipe makes a big batch—enough to keep the cookie jar filled for at least three days! Because they're fancy, dainty, absolutely yummy, for teas, showers and wedding receptions. Because they're big, satisfying and nourishing—a perfect snack for a hungry field crew or children who prefer an old-fashioned cookie with a glass of milk after school. Because the cookies stay crisp. Or stay moist. Because they pack and travel well to college dormitories and army camps. But mostly because someone in the family says, "These are good."

Whatever flavor your family likes best: chocolate, lemon, butterscotch . . . whatever type of cookie you like to make: bars, drops or cut-outs, look in this chapter for the recipes our cookbook users voted "best-ever."

I'd like to have a nickel for every Fudge Nut Bar I've made over the years—I would be rich and I feel rich indeed from all the grandchildren's compliments. (New York) □My four teen-agers consider it a special treat when I pack these fudge bars— I always tuck in extras for them to share with their friends. (Iowa) □I'm 12 years old and have been making these cookies for two years. My brother likes them as a snack before he does chores. (South Dakota) □I wrap each bar individually to sell at church bazaars—we always make a good profit. (Minnesota)

FUDGE NUT BARS

1 c. butter or regular margarine
2 c. brown sugar, firmly packed
2 eggs
2 tsp. vanilla
2½ c. sifted flour
1 tsp. baking soda
1 tsp. salt
3 c. quick-cooking rolled oats
1 (12 oz.) pkg. semisweet chocolate
   pieces
1 c. sweetened condensed milk
2 tblsp. butter or regular margarine
½ tsp. salt
1 c. chopped walnuts
2 tsp. vanilla

Cream together 1 c. butter and sugar in bowl until light and fluffy. Beat in eggs and 2 tsp. vanilla.

Sift together flour, baking soda and 1 tsp. salt. Add with oats to creamed mixture; mix well.

Combine chocolate pieces, condensed milk, 2 tblsp. butter and ½ tsp. salt in double boiler top. Place over hot water; stir until melted. Remove from heat. Add walnuts and 2 tsp. vanilla. Spread two thirds of dough in greased 15½x10½x1-inch jelly roll pan. Cover with fudge filling. Dot with remaining dough, swirling over filling.

Bake in 350° oven 25 minutes or until done. Cool in pan on rack. Cut 2x1-inch bars. Makes 72.

If you could see the smile on my husband's face when he comes in from the field and finds a pan of Brownies for a Crowd—you'd be convinced it's a very special recipe in our house. (North Dakota) □I've served these at our Flying Farmer Meetings. I keep copies of the recipe on hand because I know they'll ask for it. (South Dakota) □On my daughter's birthday, I bake a batch of these brownies to send to school. There's never a crumb left. (Pennsylvania) □This brownie recipe has made the rounds in our family. It has been served at picnics, holiday dinners, christenings, weddings. (Michigan)

BROWNIES FOR A CROWD

½ c. butter or regular margarine
1 c. sugar
4 eggs
1 tsp. vanilla
1 (1 lb.) can chocolate syrup (1½ c.)
1 c. sifted flour
½ tsp. baking powder
¼ tsp. salt
½ c. chopped walnuts
6 tblsp. butter or regular margarine
6 tblsp. milk
1 c. sugar
½ c. semisweet chocolate pieces
1 tsp. vanilla

Cream together ½ c. butter and 1 c. sugar until light and fluffy. Beat in eggs and 1 tsp. vanilla; blend well. Stir in chocolate syrup.

Sift together flour, baking powder and salt. Stir into chocolate mixture. Add walnuts. Pour into well-greased 15½x10½x1-inch jelly roll pan.

Bake in 350° oven 22 minutes or until done. Cool in pan on rack. Combine 6 tblsp. butter, milk and 1 c. sugar in saucepan. Bring to a boil; boil 30 seconds. Remove from heat. Add chocolate pieces and 1 tsp. vanilla; stir until mixture thickens slightly. Spread over brownies; cut in 2½x1½-inch bars. Makes 60.

Pumpkin Pie Squares are especially good to serve to large groups. In fact, my husband likes them better than his favorite pumpkin pie. They've become a regular at our Thanksgiving dinner. (Virginia)   □We raise pumpkins and get tired of pumpkin pie. These squares are a delicious change. (Kansas) □Tastes much like a pumpkin pie without the bother and fuss. (Minnesota)   □We harvest our own pumpkins so I always cook and freeze plenty to have on hand for these scrumptious squares. (Illinois)   □Our family gatherings are huge. Until I found your recipe for Pumpkin Pie Squares, I made two or three pies. Now just one recipe makes enough. (Iowa)

PUMPKIN PIE SQUARES

1 c. sifted flour
½ c. quick-cooking rolled oats
½ c. brown sugar, firmly packed
½ c. butter or regular margarine
1 (1 lb.) can pumpkin (2 c.)
1 (13½ oz.) can evaporated milk
2 eggs
¾ c. sugar
½ tsp. salt
1 tsp. ground cinnamon
½ tsp. ground ginger
¼ tsp. ground cloves
½ c. chopped pecans
½ c. brown sugar, firmly packed
2 tblsp. butter or regular margarine

Combine flour, oats, ½ c. brown sugar and ½ c. butter; mix until crumbly. Press into ungreased 13x9x2-inch pan. Bake in 350° oven 15 minutes.

Combine pumpkin, evaporated milk, eggs, sugar, salt, cinnamon, ginger and cloves in bowl; blend well. Pour into crust. Bake in 350° oven 20 minutes.

Combine pecans, ½ c. brown sugar and 2 tblsp. butter; sprinkle over pumpkin filling. Return to oven and bake 15 to 20 minutes or until filling is set. Cool in pan on rack and cut in 2-inch (about) squares. Makes 2 dozen.

Pumpkin Pie Squares—recipe, page 268

The very first recipe I made after I was married was your Lemon-Coconut Squares. Since then they have become my specialty. It's become a tradition for me to bring my lemon squares to family get-togethers. I've often wondered just how many batches I have made—my recipe card is spattered and worn. It doesn't matter, I know the recipe by heart. (Ohio) □My reputation as a good cook began when I appeared at a church supper with several batches of lemon squares. (Indiana) □These lemon squares are perfect. (Iowa)

LEMON-COCONUT SQUARES

1½ c. sifted flour
½ c. brown sugar, firmly packed
½ c. butter or regular margarine
2 eggs, beaten
1 c. brown sugar, firmly packed
1½ c. flaked or shredded coconut
1 c. chopped walnuts
2 tblsp. flour
½ tsp. baking powder
¼ tsp. salt
½ tsp. vanilla
1 c. sifted confectioners sugar
1 tblsp. melted butter or regular
 margarine
Juice of 1 lemon

Combine 1½ c. flour, ½ c. brown sugar and ½ c. butter in bowl; mix well. Press mixture in well-greased 13x9x2-inch baking pan. Bake in 275° oven 10 minutes.

Combine eggs, 1 c. brown sugar, coconut, walnuts, 2 tblsp. flour, baking powder, salt and vanilla. Spread on crust. Bake in 350° oven 20 minutes.

While warm, spread with confectioners sugar combined with 1 tblsp. melted butter and lemon juice. Cut in squares. Cool in pan on rack. Makes about 2 dozen.

Twice a month I make a batch of Corn Flake Cookies. They last two days. My children's friends appear on the scene as soon as the cookies are cooling on the rack. My husband reminds me to save some for him. (Kansas) □My grandchildren's most requested cookie. I often serve them with fresh peach sundaes. The brown sugar flavor is delectable. (Indiana) □A wonderful go-with-coffee cookie. All my guests want the recipe. One woman who couldn't read English watched as I mixed a batch so she could make them for her family. Even my husband who doesn't like coconut reaches for these cookies— he says they are good in spite of the coconut. (Wyoming)

CORN FLAKE COOKIES

2 c. sifted flour
1 tsp. baking soda
½ tsp. salt
½ tsp. baking powder
1¼ c. shortening
1 c. sugar
1 c. brown sugar, firmly packed
2 eggs, well beaten
1 tsp. vanilla
2 c. flaked or shredded coconut
2 c. corn flakes

Sift together flour, baking soda, salt and baking powder.

Cream together shortening and sugars in bowl until light. Add eggs and vanilla.

Add dry ingredients to creamed mixture; mix well. Add coconut and corn flakes . Drop by spoonfuls on greased baking sheet, 1½ inches apart.

Bake in 350° oven 8 to 10 minutes or until delicately browned. Remove from baking sheets; cool on racks. Makes 8 dozen.

I've tried dozens of oatmeal cookie recipes—Oatmeal/Coconut Crisps outshine them all. (Illinios) □My younger brother bakes a batch of these a week—he loves them and never lets the cookie jar get empty. (Nebraska) □Since there are seven children in the family, this is a great recipe for me. (Iowa) □When my three children were home I could never make e- nough of these cookies. When they went to college, they would take a huge box of these cookies back to the dormitory. Each year, their college friends would remind them to bring the oat- meal cookies. (Virginia) □I freeze big bags of Oatmeal Crisps—a treasure of a recipe. (Idaho) □A dandy cookie rec- ipe. It makes a big batch and dough stores well in the refriger- ator if I am too busy to bake them all. My husband tells me that I sure am a good cook when I bake these for him. (Washington)

OATMEAL/COCONUT CRISPS

2 c. butter or regular margarine
2 c. brown sugar, firmly packed
2 c. sugar
2 tsp. vanilla
4 eggs
3 c. sifted flour
2 tsp. salt
2 tsp. baking soda
6 c. quick-cooking rolled oats
1½ c. flaked coconut

Cream together butter and sugars in bowl until fluffy with electric mixer at medium speed. Add va- nilla and then eggs, one at a time, beating after each addition.

Sift together flour, salt and baking soda. Add to creamed mixture; blend well. Stir in rolled oats and coconut. Drop by teaspoonfuls about 2 inches apart on well-greased baking sheets.

Bake in 350° oven 10 to 15 minutes. Remove from baking sheets. Cool on racks. Makes 14 dozen.

I've never found a child who didn't like Oatmeal Chippers. (Vermont) □Men love this hearty cookie. I make large-sized ones loaded with walnuts. (Missouri) □My family's favorite cookie was chocolate chip until the day I made these oatmeal cookies. They even taste good frosty cold from the freezer. (Indiana) □The cinnamon and nutmeg add a different flavor to these cookies. (Iowa) □I sometimes substitute multicolored chocolate candies for the chips. Youngsters like the colored candies poking out of the cookies—have sold out at bake sales in 30 minutes. (California)

OATMEAL CHIPPERS

½ c. butter or regular margarine
½ c. shortening
1 c. sugar
1 c. brown sugar, firmly packed
2 eggs
1 tsp. vanilla
2 c. sifted flour
1 tsp. baking soda
1 tsp. salt
1 tsp. ground cinnamon
1 tsp. ground nutmeg
2 c. quick-cooking rolled oats
1 (6 oz.) pkg. semisweet chocolate
   pieces
1 c. chopped walnuts

Cream together butter and shortening in bowl with electric mixer at medium speed. Add sugars gradually, beating until light and fluffy. Beat in eggs and vanilla.

Sift together flour, baking soda, salt, cinnamon and nutmeg. Blend in sifted dry ingredients, mixing thoroughly. Stir in oats, chocolate pieces and nuts. Drop by rounded teaspoonfuls about 2 inches apart onto greased baking sheet.

Bake in 375° oven 9 to 12 minutes. Remove from baking sheets; cool on racks. Makes 8 dozen.

I made a recipe of Best-Ever Butterscotch Cookies and brought them to work as an office treat. The men liked them so well, they took up a collection and asked me to make another batch the next day. (Ohio) □If you like a soft cookie with a rich buttery flavor, this cookie is it. The Brown Butter Frosting makes it just scrumptious eating. (Wyoming) □The frosting makes them extra-fancy for parties. (Iowa) □We like soft cookies. These are so easy to make and the taste is fantastic. I make them extra big for the family and small and dainty for special occasions. (Pennsylvania) □A wonderful Christmas gift along with a copy of the recipe—every friend who has received my gift has added this cookie to her Christmas cookie list the next year. (Maryland)

BEST-EVER
BUTTERSCOTCH COOKIES

1 tblsp. vinegar
1 c. evaporated milk (about)
½ c. butter or regular margarine
1½ c. brown sugar, firmly packed
2 eggs
1 tsp. vanilla
2½ c. sifted flour
1 tsp. baking soda
½ tsp. baking powder
½ tsp. salt
⅔ c. chopped walnuts or pecans
Brown Butter Frosting (recipe
   follows)
Walnut or pecan halves

Put vinegar in a 1-cup measure; add enough evaporated milk to make 1 c. and set aside.

Beat butter in bowl with electric mixer at medium speed until light; add brown sugar and beat until mixture is light and fluffy. Beat in eggs and vanilla, blending thoroughly.

Sift together flour, baking soda, baking powder and salt.

Stir evaporated milk and add alternately with dry ingredients to creamed mixture. Stir in chopped walnuts. Drop rounded tablespoonfuls of dough, about 2½ inches apart, onto greased baking sheet.

Bake in 350° oven 10 to 12 minutes or until lightly browned and barely firm to touch. Remove from baking sheets; cool on racks. When cool, spread with Brown Butter Frosting and press a walnut or pecan half in each cookie. Makes 5 dozen.

BROWN BUTTER FROSTING

½ c. butter
2 c. sifted confectioners sugar
2 to 4 tblsp. boiling water

Melt butter in small saucepan. Cook over medium heat, stirring constantly, until butter stops bubbling and is nut-brown in color (do not scorch).

Add confectioners sugar and boiling water, a little at a time, beating well after each addition. Beat until smooth and of spreading consistency.

Oatmeal/Molasses Cookies—recipe, page 277

My daughter owned a small sandwich shop and sold these big Oatmeal/Molasses Cookies for a quarter apiece—they were always a sell-out. Now she works at a lake resort restaurant and the fishermen buy them by the dozens. (Oregon)   □These are our vacation cookies. I make them extra-large, about four inches in diameter—hungry campers welcome them for dessert. (Wisconsin)   □We call these cookies our backpackers. I make six-inch cookies—they are filling and nourishing for long hikes. (Montana)   □Last year I made Oatmeal/Molasses Cookies at Christmastime—cut them in the shape of gingerbread men and hung them on our tree. (Indiana)

OATMEAL/MOLASSES COOKIES

8½ c. sifted flour
2 tblsp. baking soda
1 tblsp. salt
8 c. quick-cooking rolled oats
2½ c. sugar
1 tblsp. ground ginger
2 c. melted shortening
2 c. light molasses
4 eggs, beaten
¼ c. hot water
3 c. seedless raisins
2 c. ground walnuts
Sugar

Reserve ½ c. flour. Sift together 8 c. flour, baking soda and salt. Mix rolled oats, sugar and ginger in a very large bowl or dishpan. Stir in shortening, molasses, eggs, hot water, dry ingredients, raisins and nuts. Work dough with hands until well mixed. Add the reserved ½ c. flour if needed.

Roll dough to ¼-inch thickness; cut with 3½-inch round cutter. Place 2 to 3 inches apart on lightly greased baking sheet. Brush with water and sprinkle with sugar.

Bake in 375° oven 8 to 10 minutes. Remove from baking sheets; cool on racks. Makes 6 dozen.

My six kids tell me that Orange/Coconut Crisps are the best in the world. I add raisins and feel I am giving my family a sweet that is nutritious. A good snack with a glass of milk. (Nebraska) □Of all the cookies that I have served at teas and taken to picnics, this rates the highest in compliments and recipe requests. (Iowa) □A cookie that keeps well and freezes beautifully providing I can get them in the freezer fast before the family polishes off the entire batch. (Texas)

ORANGE/COCONUT CRISPS

2 eggs
⅔ c. cooking oil
1 c. sugar
¼ c. frozen orange juice
   concentrate, thawed
2½ c. sifted flour
2 tsp. baking powder
½ tsp. salt
1 c. cookie coconut

Beat eggs with a fork or a wire whisk in a medium bowl. Stir in oil and sugar; beat until mixture thickens. Stir in orange concentrate (do not dilute).

Sift together flour, baking powder and salt. Add dry ingredients and coconut to egg mixture. Stir to mix well.

Drop by teaspoonfuls about 2 inches apart onto ungreased baking sheet. Flatten each cookie with the bottom of a drinking glass, coated with cooking oil and dipped in sugar.

Bake in 400° oven 8 to 10 minutes or until golden brown. Remove from baking sheets and cool on racks. Makes about 3 dozen.

A rich chewy brownie that tastes just like the brownies Mother used to make. (Alaska) □With four lunches to pack daily, this Brownie recipe is quick and easy to make and pleases the family. It's also my standby to serve at card parties, with a big pot of coffee. (New York) □I have three sons who like brownies better than anything in the world. They think Mom is the greatest when I make them a batch of their favorite sweet. (Nebraska) □When my husband was in the Service he always looked forward to a box of these brownies. (Michigan)

BROWNIES

1 c. sugar
2 eggs
2 (1 oz.) squares unsweetened
   chocolate
½ c. butter or regular margarine
½ c. unsifted flour
1 tsp. vanilla
½ c. chopped walnuts
1 c. sugar
1 egg, beaten
2 tblsp. light cream
2 (1 oz.) squares unsweetened
   chocolate
2 tblsp. butter or regular margarine
1 tsp. vanilla

Beat together 1 c. sugar and 2 eggs in bowl with electric mixer at medium speed until blended. Combine 2 squares chocolate and ½ c. butter in saucepan. Heat over low heat until melted, stirring constantly. Remove from heat. Blend into egg mixture. Add flour and vanilla; mix well. Stir in walnuts. Spread in greased 8-inch square baking pan.

Bake in 350° oven 25 to 35 minutes or until done. Cool in pan on rack.

Combine remaining ingredients in saucepan. Heat over low heat until melted. Remove from heat; stir until thick enough to spread. Spread over brownies. Cut in 2-inch squares. Makes 16.

One taste of a Lemon Love Note cookie and you must have another. (Maine) □A cookie with a marvelous buttery-lemony flavor. (California) □I always make these for showers and wedding receptions, cutting them into dainty bite-sized pieces. (New Hampshire) □I'm a school librarian. When I first tasted the Lemon Love Notes at a friend's home, I immediately ordered one copy of your book for me and one for the library. Since then many women have come in and copied the recipe—it's superior. (Maryland) □My daughter made these cookies and served them at a 4-H meeting. Everyone wanted the recipe immediately—they loved the tangy lemon flavor. (Massachusetts)

LEMON LOVE NOTES

½ c. butter or regular margarine
1 c. sifted flour
¼ c. confectioners sugar
1 c. sugar
2 tblsp. flour
½ tsp. baking powder
2 eggs, beaten
2 tblsp. lemon juice
2 tsp. grated lemon rind
Confectioners sugar

Combine butter, 1 c. flour and confectioners sugar in bowl; mix until crumbly. Press into ungreased 8-inch square pan.

Bake in 350° oven 8 minutes or until golden brown. Cool in pan on rack.

Combine sugar, 2 tblsp. flour and baking powder in bowl. Add eggs, lemon juice and rind. Mix well. Pour evenly over baked, cooled crust.

Bake in 350° oven 25 minutes. (Top puffs up in baking, but falls in cooling.) Cool in pan on rack and cut in 2-inch squares. Sprinkle with confectioners sugar. Makes 16.

I often bake Saucepan Brownies for bake sales—they are easy to fix and always sell fast. (Indiana)   □My family is crazy about these cookies—all my married daughters have the recipe and bake them often for their youngsters. (New York)   □We love brownies. This recipe is a timesaver as all the ingredients are mixed in one pan. (North Carolina)   □When there is no dessert and I'm short on time, I reach for this brownie recipe. It goes well with ice cream and is also good served warm from the oven—a moist, fudgy brownie. (Nebraska)   □My favorite brownie to serve with a milk punch at committee meetings. So quick and easy to fix. I usually double the recipe and bake in a 13x9x1-inch pan. (Oregon)

SAUCEPAN BROWNIES

½ c. butter or regular margarine
2 (1 oz.) squares unsweetened
  chocolate
1 c. sugar
½ c. sifted flour
1 tsp. baking powder
1 tsp. vanilla
½ c. chopped walnuts
2 eggs
Confectioners sugar

Melt together butter and chocolate in saucepan. Remove from heat. Stir in sugar, flour, baking powder, vanilla and walnuts. Add eggs; beat thoroughly. Spread in greased 9-inch square baking pan.

Bake in 350° oven 30 minutes or until done. Cool in pan on rack. Dust with confectioners sugar and cut in squares. Makes 1½ dozen.
Note: Cut in large squares; top with vanilla ice cream and chocolate sauce.

For years I baked Crackle-Top Ginger Cookies for my ten grandchildren to pack into their lunchboxes. Now they bake their own and pass this recipe onto their friends. (Oregon) □A cookie that truly does melt in your mouth. My husband says they are dandy to tuck into his pockets as they don't crumble. Grandpa says they are just like his Grandmother used to make years ago in Louisiana when he was a little boy—a true family favorite. (Wisconsin) □I bake loads of cookies of every description, but this crispy ginger cookie is the one my family asks me to make the most often. (Vermont)

CRACKLE-TOP GINGER COOKIES

1 c. shortening
2 c. brown sugar, firmly packed
1 egg, well beaten
1 c. molasses
4 c. sifted flour
2 tsp. baking soda
2 tsp. ground ginger
½ tsp. salt
1 tsp. vanilla
1 tsp. lemon extract
Sugar

Cream together shortening and brown sugar in bowl with electric mixer at medium speed until light and fluffy. Blend in egg and molasses.

Sift together flour, baking soda, ginger and salt. Gradually add dry ingredients to creamed mixture. Add vanilla and lemon extract. Chill 4 hours.

Dough will be soft. With lightly floured hands, shape into balls about 1½ inches in diameter. Place on greased baking sheet.

Bake in 350° oven 12 to 15 minutes or until brown. Sprinkle with sugar. Remove from baking sheet and cool on racks. Makes 2½ dozen.

We like chewy cookies and these Oatmeal/Chocolate Bars are extra-chewy. And they make a great big batch—necessary in our house because they disappear so fast. (Michigan) □Just taste these cookies once and you will agree they are delicious—don't overbake or they will dry out. (Idaho)   □This recipe makes lots of cookies. They are moist with an interesting combination of flavors. Our daughter has made these so many times for her guests and for meetings that now they are known as "Kathy's cookies." (Illinois)   □I have four children who pre-fer cookies to any other sweet. This is a popular recipe as it makes a big batch in a short time. (Wisconsin)

OATMEAL/CHOCOLATE BARS

1½ c. brown sugar, firmly packed
¾ c. sugar
1 c. shortening
3 eggs
1 tsp. vanilla
2¼ c. sifted flour
1 tsp. salt
1 tsp. baking soda
1½ tsp. ground cinnamon
¾ c. milk
4 c. quick-cooking rolled oats
1 (12 oz.) pkg. semisweet chocolate
   pieces

Cream together sugars and shortening until light and fluffy. Beat in eggs and vanilla.

Sift together flour, salt, baking soda and cinna-mon. Add to creamed mixture along with milk. Stir in oats and chocolate pieces. Spread batter in greased 15½x10½x1-inch jelly roll pan.

Bake in 350° oven about 30 minutes or until done. Cool in pan on rack. While warm, cut in 2x1-inch bars. Makes about 6 dozen.

I baked Chocolate Macaroons and took them to our local school carnival. My husband walked right behind me and bought them all. (Minnesota) □A must-make on my Christmas cookie list. I sometimes vary the recipe by adding coconut, nuts or Rice Krispies. (Utah) □The very top favorite cookie with my husband, children and hired men. (Vermont) □A cookie that never fails to please. Looks pretty, tastes extra-good and is a bit different from most cookies. (New Mexico) □When my children have a piano recital they always ask me to make those good chewy chocolate cookies to serve at refreshment time. Good plain or with nuts. (New Mexico)

CHOCOLATE MACAROONS

½ c. shortening
4 (1 oz.) squares unsweetened
   chocolate
2 c. sifted flour
2 tsp. baking powder
½ tsp. salt
2 c. sugar
4 eggs
2 tsp. vanilla
Confectioners sugar

Combine shortening and chocolate in saucepan. Heat over low heat, stirring constantly, until melted. Sift together flour, baking powder and salt.

Add sugar to chocolate mixture, stirring until smooth. Add eggs, one at a time, beating well after each addition.

Add flour mixture; blend thoroughly. Beat in vanilla. Chill dough 2 to 3 hours.

Dip out rounded teaspoons of dough; form into small balls. Roll each in confectioners sugar. Place on greased baking sheets.

Bake in 375° oven about 10 minutes. (Do not overbake. Cookies should be soft when taken from oven.) Remove from baking sheets; cool on racks. Makes 5 to 6 dozen.

Grandma's Soft Sugar Cookies should be in every recipe file—they are outstanding. (Pennsylvania) □Wouldn't be without a batch of these sugar cookies in my freezer for unexpected company. (Nebraska) □A lovely, soft old-fashioned kind of sugar cookie that holds its shape during baking—my grandchildren always want me to make these when they come to visit. (Iowa) □Never fail to make a hit with children at bake sales—they stand on tiptoe and say, "One sugar cookie, please." The next day many mothers call and ask me for the recipe. (Ohio)

GRANDMA'S SOFT SUGAR COOKIES

1 c. sugar
1 c. brown sugar, firmly packed
½ c. butter
½ c. shortening
2 eggs
1 tsp. vanilla
½ tsp. lemon extract
3½ c. sifted flour
2 tsp. baking powder
1 tsp. cream of tartar
1 tsp. ground nutmeg
¾ tsp. salt
¾ tsp. baking soda
1 c. buttermilk
Sugar
Raisins

Beat together sugars, butter and shortening until fluffy. Beat in eggs, vanilla and lemon extract.

Sift together flour, baking powder, cream of tartar, nutmeg, salt and baking soda. Add alternately with buttermilk to creamed mixture. Drop by tablespoonfuls 2½ inches apart on greased baking sheet. Sprinkle with sugar and place a raisin in center of each cookie.

Bake in 400° oven 10 minutes or until done. Remove from baking sheets; cool on racks. Makes 48.

Danish Apple Bars look and taste like a recipe I received from a good Hungarian cook—these are much simpler to make. I use dry bread crumbs instead of corn flakes for the topping. (Arkansas)   □My husband's grandmother is renowned for her strudel. When I made and served this to her she liked it as well as her complicated recipe. (Wisconsin)   □A recipe everyone raves about—the dough is so easy, even a beginner can master it. (Iowa)   □This apple dessert makes lots of helpings and looks more special than a regular apple pie. (New Jersey)

DANISH APPLE BARS

3 c. sifted flour
1 tsp. salt
1 c. shortening
1 egg yolk, beaten
Milk
1 c. crushed corn flakes
8 large apples, pared and sliced
  (8 c.)
1 c. sugar
1 tsp. ground cinnamon
1 egg white, beaten until stiff
1 c. sifted confectioners sugar
3 tblsp. water
1 tsp. vanilla

Sift together flour and salt. Cut in shortening until crumbly. Add enough milk to egg yolk to make ½ c. Add to flour mixture; mix until moistened.

Divide dough almost in half. Roll out larger half. Line 15½x10½x1-inch jelly roll pan with dough. Sprinkle with corn flakes; top with apples. Combine sugar and cinnamon; sprinkle over apples. Roll out other half of dough to fit top. Cut vents; seal edges. Spread egg white over crust.

Bake in 375° oven 1 hour or until golden. Cool in pan on rack. Combine confectioners sugar, water and vanilla; mix well. Spread on bars while warm. Cut in 16 bars. Makes 16 servings.

OTHER DESSERTS

OTHER DESSERTS

HOMEMADE VANILLA ICE CREAM
VANILLA ICE CREAM
STRAWBERRY PARFAIT RING
RHUBARB CRUNCH
MARIELLA'S ICE CREAM
RASPBERRY/VANILLA CLOUD
VIRGINIA APPLE PUDDING
OLD-TIME APPLE DUMPLINGS
BLUEBERRY TREAT
RASPBERRY TORTE
RASPBERRY SWIRL
APPLE PIE PIZZA
PERFECT BAKED CUSTARD
LEMON PUDDING CAKE
CHERRY CRUMB CAKE

Delicious Desserts

The votes for desserts among FARM JOURNAL cookbook devotees were sufficient to put sweets in a close finish with all other categories combined. This is no surprise to FARM JOURNAL editors. How often we've shared a meal in a farm home, mindful to save room for the sweet ending we knew would be offered. Who could resist a rosy dish of sweet-tart rhubarb, the first of the season? Or Old-Time Apple Dumplings, with thick cream to pour over?

In a country home, even a coffee visit means something good to munch on, while an evening of cards, conversation or community work with your neighbors will virtually guarantee a second dessert before you all go home to bed. Such occasions give good cooks the excuse (if they need it) to fix something so delightful their friends will ask for the recipe.

Because desserts got such an overwhelming proportion of the votes, we divided them into four chapters: Cakes, Pies, Cookies—and this one which includes all the other Delicious Desserts our readers like to make and serve. Here are the homemade ice creams, puddings, tortes, custards and chilled or frozen fruit desserts which, our voters say, consistently win praise.

Vanilla ice cream, churned on the back porch, is Number One. But we leave it to you to decide which one of the three versions nominated your family will like best—you can read the comments with each recipe.

Farm women who have orchards and berry patches favored fruit desserts. They nominated apple recipes in all four dessert categories—a reflection of the popularity and year-round abundance of this favorite and plentiful fruit. And they singled out raspberries for attention—Raspberry Swirl was second only to ice cream in this chapter and we counted no fewer than three raspberry desserts among the top favorites. A real treat for city friends, they explain. Rounding out the list are desserts made with strawberries, blueberries, cherries and rhubarb.

We predict you won't be able to finish this chapter before you head for the kitchen.

When we received an ice cream freezer as a gift several years ago, we began experimenting with recipes. No more. This recipe for Homemade Vanilla Ice Cream is the family favorite now. At our family gatherings, we always make the ice cream. (Iowa) □During the hot summer months, we make this ice cream at least once a week. It's so rich and creamy. (Oregon) □We don't need to buy ice cream powder or gelatin, we can make this ice cream on the spur of the moment. (Kansas) □When we serve this ice cream to our youth group, it quickly disappears. (Missouri)

HOMEMADE VANILLA ICE CREAM

1 qt. milk
2 c. sugar
¼ c. flour
½ tsp. salt
4 eggs, slightly beaten
1 tblsp. vanilla
1½ qts. light cream or dairy half-and-half

Scald milk in 3-qt. saucepan. Mix sugar, flour and salt in small bowl. Add enough hot milk to sugar-flour mixture to make a thin paste. Stir paste into hot milk. Cook over low heat, stirring constantly, until mixture thickens slightly, about 15 minutes.

Add hot mixture gradually to beaten eggs. Then add back to saucepan. Cook over low heat, stirring constantly, until mixture thickens slightly, about 2 minutes (do not cook longer or eggs may curdle).

Cool quickly in refrigerator. Do not allow mixture to cool at room temperature.

Add vanilla and light cream to cooled mixture. Pour into 1-gal. freezer can, filling only two-thirds full. Freeze following usual procedure for crank or electric ice cream freezer. Makes 1 gallon.

Vanilla Ice Cream—recipe, page 292

Homemade Vanilla Ice Cream—recipe, page 290

My husband makes this Vanilla Ice Cream often. He received so many compliments this summer when he added fresh bananas—it was extra-special. (Missouri) □A recipe we can rely on. It has become a natural for our quiet Sunday summer afternoons. The whole family looks forward to a bowl of creamy smooth ice cream. Sometimes we top it with crushed fresh fruit of the season. (Iowa) □The grape variation is a special treat. So many of my guests never had grape ice cream before . . . they always want a copy of the recipe. (Wisconsin)

VANILLA ICE CREAM

2 tblsp. unflavored gelatin
½ c. cold milk
1½ c. milk
2 c. sugar
¼ tsp. salt
1 c. milk
6 eggs
1½ qts. light cream
1 (3¾ oz.) pkg. vanilla instant
   pudding
5 tsp. vanilla

Soften gelatin in ½ c. milk in bowl. Scald 1½ c. milk in saucepan. Stir in gelatin mixture until it dissolves. Add sugar and salt, stirring until dissolved. Add 1 c. milk. Remove from heat.

Beat eggs at high speed of electric mixer 5 minutes. Add light cream, pudding mix, vanilla and gelatin mixture. Pour into 1-gal. freezer can. Freeze, following usual procedure for crank or electric ice cream freezer. Makes 3½ quarts.

Grape: Substitute 3 c. grape juice for milk. Proceed as directed, reducing light cream to 5 c. and sugar to 1¼ c.; omit vanilla. Add the juice of 1 lemon.

Cinnamon: Slowly melt ⅔ c. cinnamon (red hot) candies with the 1½ c. milk. Proceed as directed, reducing sugar to 1¼ c. and vanilla to 1 tblsp.

Coffee Walnut: Add ¼ c. instant coffee with pudding mix. Reduce vanilla to 1 tblsp. After ice cream is frozen, stir in 1 c. chopped, toasted walnuts.

Peppermint Stick: Melt ½ c. crushed peppermint stick candy with the 1½ c. milk. Proceed as directed, reducing sugar to 1¼ c. and vanilla to 1 tblsp. After ice cream is frozen, stir in ½ c. crushed peppermint stick candy.

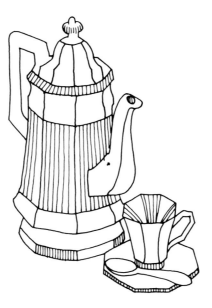

Perfect dessert for Christmas dinner—Strawberry Parfait Ring is so pretty and so luscious. Everyone asks what ingredients are in the recipe because it tastes so good. I often make it in different shaped molds to fit the particular holiday. (North Dakota)   □So lovely in individual ring or angel food cake pans. Decorate each with a puff of whipped cream and a sprig of fresh mint. (Oregon)   □Sometimes I decorate this dessert with assorted pastel-colored candy mints . . . adds a different touch. (Kansas)

STRAWBERRY PARFAIT RING

1 c. sugar
⅓ c. boiling water
Red food color
4 egg whites
1 tsp. vanilla
⅛ tsp. salt
2 c. heavy cream, whipped
Strawberries (about 1½ qts.)
Flaked or shredded coconut
1 c. heavy cream, whipped

Combine sugar and water in saucepan. Cook over medium heat until syrup spins a thread (235°). Add a few drops of red food color.

Beat egg whites in large bowl until stiff; gradually add hot syrup. Continue beating until cool and light. Add vanilla and salt.

Fold in whipped cream. Pour into a 2-qt. ring mold and freeze. (Directions for individual rings follow.)

At serving time, unmold and fill center of ring with strawberries. Sprinkle top of ring with coconut. Border the ring with puffs of whipped cream, one for each serving. Makes 12 to 16 servings.

Individual Strawberry Parfait Rings: Freeze parfait mixture in individual angel food pans or ring molds. To serve, turn out on dessert plates and fill centers with fresh or frozen strawberries. (Other berries or sliced peaches may be used.)

I serve Rhubarb Crunch to every group and club that meets in my home, and I am always asked for the recipe. The only change I make is to add some red food coloring to make it more colorful. (Ohio)   □A great way to use up surplus rhubarb. I usually freeze several quarts of rhubarb to make this dessert during the cold winter months . . . a nice change from rhubarb pie. (New York)   □Springtime means lots of requests for this recipe. It is especially luscious topped with a spoonful of either strawberry or raspberry/vanilla ice cream. (Iowa)

RHUBARB CRUNCH

1 c. sifted flour
¾ c. quick rolled oats
1 c. brown sugar, firmly packed
½ c. melted butter or regular
   margarine
1 tsp. ground cinnamon
4 c. diced fresh rhubarb
1 c. sugar
2 tblsp. cornstarch
1 c. water
1 tsp. vanilla
Sweetened whipped cream (optional)

Combine flour, oats, brown sugar, butter and cinnamon in bowl. Mix until crumbly. Press half of crumbs in greased 9-inch layer pan.

Cover with rhubarb. Combine sugar, cornstarch, water and vanilla in small saucepan. Cook, stirring, until thick and clear. Pour over rhubarb. Top with remaining crumbs.

Bake in 350° oven 1 hour. Cut in squares. Serve warm, plain or topped with whipped cream. Makes 8 servings.

Mariella's Ice Cream is the most fantastic tasting ice cream. There's never any left to store in the freezer. (Ohio) □We're dairy farmers so we always have extra milk and cream to turn into homemade ice cream. This is my favorite ice cream, easy to make and doesn't crystallize like so many ice creams. And it's not too rich. (California) □No one minds cranking the freezer when I announce I'm going to make the family's favorite ice cream. (Idaho) □We like an old-fashioned cooked type of ice cream like this—it's our birthday ice cream. (Kansas) □Delicious! Especially the strawberry variation. (Michigan) □Every summer we have ice cream socials. Each family brings a freezer and ice cream ingredients. Mariella's always gets eaten first. (Washington)

MARIELLA'S ICE CREAM

1 qt. milk, scalded
4 eggs, beaten
2½ c. sugar
2½ to 3 c. heavy cream
1 qt. cold milk
2 tblsp. vanilla
¼ tsp. salt
3 drops lemon extract

Stir 1 qt. hot milk into eggs and sugar in bowl. Return to saucepan. Cook over low heat until thickened, stirring constantly; cool.

Add heavy cream, 1 qt. milk, vanilla, salt and lemon extract to milk mixture; stir until smooth. Pour into 1-gal. freezer can. Freeze, following usual procedure for crank or electric ice cream freezer. Makes about 1 gallon.

Chocolate: Stir 1 (5½ oz.) can chocolate syrup into vanilla mixture.

Strawberry: Mix 3 (10 oz.) pkgs. frozen strawberries, thawed, and ½ c. sugar; stir into vanilla mixture. Add red food color for pink ice cream.

Raspberry/Vanilla Cloud is always the grand finale to our Christmas dinner . . . light eating after a heavy turkey meal. (Minnesota)   □I serve this to my family year round, but we like it especially in the winter—it's so colorful and pretty. (Kansas) □Even fussy eaters who turn up their noses at new recipes are willing to try this. After the first spoonful, the rest disappears in a hurry. Any leftover sauce is yummy over angel food cake or vanilla ice cream. (California)

RASPBERRY/VANILLA CLOUD

1⅔ c. graham cracker crumbs
¼ c. sugar
1 tsp. ground cinnamon
⅓ c. melted butter or regular
   margarine
½ c. sugar
¼ c. flour
1 pkg. unflavored gelatin
½ tsp. salt
1¾ c. milk
3 egg whites
¼ tsp. cream of tartar
½ c. sugar
1 tsp. vanilla
½ c. heavy cream, whipped
Raspberry Sauce (recipe follows)

Combine graham crumbs, ¼ c. sugar, cinnamon and butter in bowl. Mix until crumbly. Press in 9-inch square baking pan.

Bake in 375° oven 4 minutes. Cool on rack.

Combine ½ c. sugar, flour, gelatin and salt in 2-qt. saucepan. Slowly stir in milk. Bring to a boil, stirring constantly. Boil for 1 minute. Cool thoroughly.

Beat egg whites with cream of tartar in bowl with electric mixer at high speed until stiff peaks form. Gradually beat in ½ c. sugar. Add vanilla.

Fold egg whites and whipped cream into cooled mixture. Turn into crust. Chill thoroughly. Cut in squares and serve topped with Raspberry Sauce. Makes 9 servings.

RASPBERRY SAUCE

**2 (10 oz.) pkgs. frozen red raspberries,
  thawed**
¼ c. sugar
2 tblsp. cornstarch
1 tblsp. lemon juice

Drain raspberries, reserving juice. Add enough water to juice to make 1½ c. Combine juice, sugar, cornstarch and lemon juice in saucepan. Cook, stirring constantly, until mixture boils. Boil 1 minute. Add raspberries and cool thoroughly.

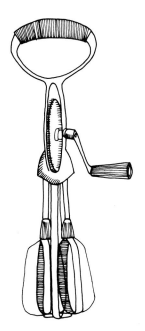

Raspberry/Vanilla Cloud—recipe, page 298

Old-Time Apple Dumplings—recipe, page 302

300

If I don't make Virginia Apple Pudding for a few weeks, my husband asks me to fix it. We have loads of apple trees and I think this recipe is one of the most interesting and unusual ways to use up all those apples. (Oregon)   □This is our favorite winter dessert—we like it with a scoop of ice cream. (Ohio) □A wonderful apple dessert—the house smells so good while it's baking. A change from the usual apple pie. (Texas)   □We like the chewy top and the tart apples underneath. Not only is the recipe good—it's quick and easy. (Washington)

VIRGINIA APPLE PUDDING

½ c. butter or regular margarine
1 c. sugar
1 c. sifted flour
2 tsp. baking powder
¼ tsp. salt
¼ tsp. ground cinnamon
1 c. milk
2 c. cooked or canned apple slices

Melt butter in 2-qt. casserole.

Combine sugar, flour, baking powder, salt and cinnamon in bowl. Mix well. Add milk and butter; blend well. Pour batter into 2-qt. casserole. Drain apples; pile in center of batter.

Bake in 375° oven 30 to 40 minutes or until batter covers fruit and crust browns. Serve warm. Makes 4 to 6 servings.

Old-Time Apple Dumplings are a success whenever I serve them. The crust never gets soggy and the flavor is delicious. (New York)   □My family especially likes these apple dumplings following a roast pork dinner. It's such an energy-saver because I can bake the main course and the dessert at the same time. (Iowa)   □The crust is so nice and flaky. Sometimes I serve the dumplings with whipped cream instead of the sauce, or with just plain half-and-half. Good that way, too. (Nebraska)

OLD-TIME APPLE DUMPLINGS

2 c. sifted flour
2 tsp. baking powder
½ tsp. salt
½ c. shortening
⅔ c. milk
6 baking apples
⅓ c. sugar
¼ tsp. ground cinnamon
1 tblsp. butter or regular margarine
Milk
Sweet Sour Sauce (recipe follows)

Sift together flour, baking powder and salt into bowl; cut in shortening until crumbs form. Stir in milk; mix until soft dough is formed.

Turn out onto lightly floured surface. Knead lightly. Roll to ⅛-inch thickness. Cut into 6 squares.

Core and pare apples. Place 1 on each square. Combine sugar and cinnamon; sprinkle in center of each apple. Add ½ tsp. butter to each.

Moisten edges of dough; press corners together over apples. Brush with milk. Place in greased 13x9x2-inch baking pan.

Bake in 350° oven 30 minutes or until crust is golden and apples are tender. Serve with Sweet Sour Sauce. Makes 6 servings.

SWEET SOUR SAUCE

⅓ c. flour
1 c. sugar
1 tsp. ground cinnamon
⅛ tsp. ground nutmeg
2 c. water
⅓ c. vinegar
⅓ c. butter or regular margarine

Combine flour, sugar, cinnamon and nutmeg in saucepan. Stir in water, vinegar and butter. Cook over low heat, stirring constantly, until thickened. Remove from heat. Serve warm sauce over warm apple dumplings.

I usually make Blueberry Treat for potluck dinners. It's easy, can be fixed ahead and is oh, so delicious. Tastes good with canned blueberries even though the recipe calls for fresh or frozen berries. (Pennsylvania) □There are three blueberry bushes in our backyard and when the fruit is ripe, Blueberry Treat appears on our table often. (Ohio) □It's a delicious dessert—also good made with crushed pineapple or raspberries. I've made all three for church bazaars and people have a hard time deciding which one they want to sample. (New Jersey)

BLUEBERRY TREAT

1⅓ c. graham cracker or vanilla
   wafer crumbs
¼ c. sifted confectioners sugar
¼ c. melted butter or regular
   margarine
2 eggs, beaten
⅓ c. sugar
1 (8 oz.) pkg. cream cheese, softened
¼ tsp. salt
1 c. fresh or frozen blueberries
½ c. sugar
2 tblsp. cornstarch
¼ tsp. salt
¼ c. water
¼ tsp. grated orange rind
1 c. fresh or frozen blueberries

Combine graham cracker crumbs, confectioners sugar and butter in bowl; mix until crumbly. Press mixture into 8-inch square baking pan.

Beat together eggs, ⅓ c. sugar, cream cheese and salt in bowl until well blended. Pour over crust.

Bake in 375° oven 20 minutes. Cool on rack.

Combine 1 c. blueberries, ½ c. sugar, cornstarch, salt, water and orange rind in saucepan. Cook over low heat, stirring constantly, until thick and clear. Arrange 1 c. blueberries over cheese layer.

Pour hot sauce over blueberry layer. Chill before serving. Makes 8 servings.

Not only is Raspberry Torte pretty, it tastes good, too. The entire family loves it and expects me to make it often. (Nebraska) □Such an easy and yet spectacular make-ahead dessert. I love to cook and entertain and try new recipes, but I still return to this dessert—a must during the holidays. (Missouri) □A dessert that's popular with all groups—both men and women ask me for the recipe. (New York) □When I entertain my club with a Scandinavian menu, Raspberry Torte ends the meal. By now most of the members have made the recipe, but they would be disappointed if I fixed another dessert. (Minnesota)

RASPBERRY TORTE

1¼ c. sifted flour
¼ c. sugar
¼ tsp. salt
1 c. butter or regular margarine
3 tblsp. cornstarch
1 c. sugar
2 (10 oz.) pkgs. frozen red
   raspberries, thawed
45 large marshmallows
1 c. milk
1 c. heavy cream, whipped

Combine flour, ¼ c. sugar and salt in bowl. Cut in butter until mixture resembles coarse crumbs. Press mixture into 13x9x2-inch baking pan.

Bake in 350° oven 15 to 18 minutes or until lightly browned. Cool in pan on rack.

Combine cornstarch and 1 c. sugar in saucepan. Add raspberries and cook, stirring constantly, until mixture comes to a boil and is clear. Cool slightly. Pour over crust. Chill.

Place marshmallows and milk in saucepan. Cook over low heat, stirring frequently, until marshmallows are melted. Cool. Fold whipped cream into marshmallow mixture. Spread evenly over chilled raspberry filling. Chill thoroughly. Cut in squares. Makes 12 servings.

My family makes frequent trips to the freezer after I have made Raspberry Swirl. (California) □We have our own raspberries, cream and eggs—this recipe is a delicious way to combine these ingredients. (South Dakota) □Raspberry Swirl tastes like homemade ice cream—a refreshing dessert for hot summer months. (Arizona) □We grow our own raspberries and this recipe is so different. I like to serve it to company. Because raspberries are expensive, this dessert is a real treat for our city friends. (Iowa) □This dessert makes a delicious dessert—a marvelous ending to a special dinner. Sometimes I substitute frozen strawberries. (Nebraska)

RASPBERRY SWIRL

¾ c. graham cracker crumbs
3 tblsp. melted butter or regular
   margarine
2 tblsp. sugar
3 eggs, separated
1 (8 oz.) pkg. cream cheese
1 c. sugar
⅛ tsp. salt
1 c. heavy cream, whipped
1 (10 oz.) pkg. frozen raspberries,
   partially thawed

Thoroughly combine crumbs, butter and 2 tblsp. sugar. Press mixture into well-greased 11x7x1½-inch baking dish. Bake in 375° oven about 8 minutes. Cool completely.

Beat egg yolks in bowl with electric mixer at high speed until thick. Add cream cheese, 1 c. sugar and salt; beat until smooth and light.

Beat egg whites until stiff peaks form. Fold egg whites and whipped cream into cheese mixture.

Puree raspberries in a mixer or blender. Gently swirl half of puree through cheese filling; spread mixture in crust. Spoon remaining puree over top; swirl with a knife. Freeze, then cover and return to freezer. Makes 6 to 8 servings.

Strawberry Parfait Ring—recipe, page 294

Raspberry Swirl—recipe, page 306

307

Apple Pie Pizza is a spectacular way to serve apples. The Cheddar cheese in the crust gives a pleasant and unusual flavor. I am never without at least one pie in the freezer, ready to heat and serve to unexpected guests. (Montana) □Served warm topped with ice cream, this apple dessert brightens an ordinary meal. (Wyoming) □My daughter has done many 4-H demonstrations of Apple Pie Pizza and she often makes it for our family of seven—we all agree this is our most favorite recipe. (Florida)

APPLE PIE PIZZA

1¼ c. sifted flour
1 tsp. salt
½ c. shortening
1 c. shredded Cheddar cheese
¼ c. ice water
½ c. powdered non-dairy "cream"
½ c. brown sugar, firmly packed
½ c. sugar
⅓ c. sifted flour
¼ tsp. salt
1 tsp. ground cinnamon
½ tsp. ground nutmeg
¼ c. butter or regular margarine
6 c. sliced pared apples, ½-inch thick
2 tblsp. lemon juice

Combine 1¼ c. flour and 1 tsp. salt in bowl. Cut in shortening until crumbly. Add cheese. Sprinkle water on top; shape into ball. Roll into 15-inch circle on floured surface. Place on baking sheet; turn up edge to form rim. Or place in 13-inch pizza pan.

Combine powdered "cream," brown sugar, sugar, ⅓ c. flour, ¼ tsp. salt, cinnamon and nutmeg; mix well. Sprinkle half of mixture over pastry. Cut butter into remaining half until crumbly; set aside. Arrange apples on crust, overlapping them in circles. Sprinkle with lemon juice; top with remaining crumbs.

Bake in 450° oven 30 minutes or until apples are tender. Delicious served warm. Makes 12 servings.

Perfect Baked Custard never weeps or separates as many custards do. I've given this recipe to friends who have never had success with baked custards. They agree this recipe is truly foolproof. (Ohio) □My party brunches always include this baked custard and my family gobbles it up, too. A nourishing dessert for the youngsters. (Pennsylvania) □Easy, delicious dessert. Not many people make a custard like this. Until I discovered this recipe, custard pie was our Saturday night dessert—it's been replaced by your Perfect Custard. (Oregon) □A light nourishing dish for old and young and especially for invalids whose appetites need tempting. (Nebraska)

PERFECT BAKED CUSTARD

6 eggs
½ to ¾ c. sugar
½ tsp. salt
4 c. hot milk
2 tsp. vanilla

Combine eggs, sugar and salt in mixing bowl. Beat just enough to blend together. Add hot milk slowly and mix well. Stir in vanilla. Strain.

Pour into 11x7x1½-inch baking dish, casserole or 8 individual custard cups. (Use cold rather than hot milk to make individual custards.) Place in a pan of hot water.

Bake in 325° oven until inserted knife comes out clean—baking dish, 45 minutes; casserole, 60 minutes; individual custards, 30 minutes. Cool. Makes 6 to 8 servings.

Lemon Pudding Cake—recipe, page 311

As a child I was served Lemon Pudding Cake in school. What a pleasure to find the recipe in your book—only it tasted twice as good. (Wisconsin)   □A much-appreciated recipe by a busy mother of three young children. A dessert that children adore and takes me little time to fix, with minimum clean-up. (Michigan)   □A dessert that's not too filling, not too sweet and not too complicated to make on a wildly busy day when I've forgotten to plan dessert for supper. (Missouri)   □A quick, easy dessert with its own baked-in creamy sauce. We love it. (Ohio)

LEMON PUDDING CAKE

4 eggs, separated
⅓ c. lemon juice
1 tsp. grated lemon rind
1 tblsp. melted butter or regular
   margarine
1½ c. sugar
½ c. sifted flour
½ tsp. salt
1½ c. milk

Beat together egg yolks, lemon juice, lemon rind and butter in bowl with rotary beater until thick and lemon-colored. Combine sugar, flour and salt. Add dry ingredients alternately with milk, beating well after each addition. Beat egg whites until stiff. Blend into yolk mixture on low speed of electric mixer. Pour mixture into 8-inch square baking dish. Set in a pan of hot water.

Bake in 350° oven 45 minutes or until golden. Cut into squares. Makes 6 to 9 servings.

How many times I've been asked for the recipe for Cherry Crumb Cake! It's so yummy guests can hardly believe how easy it is to prepare. (Iowa) □Especially good served warm from the oven with a dollop of whipped cream. I often substitute other pie fillings for the cherry . . . every one is a favorite. (Wisconsin) □This bright red dessert always gets raves when I serve it, especially on a cold, wintry day. (Massachusetts)

CHERRY CRUMB CAKE

2 c. sifted flour
1 c. sugar
2 tsp. baking powder
½ tsp. salt
½ c. butter or regular margarine
1 egg
1 (1 lb. 8 oz.) jar cherry pie filling

Sift together flour, sugar, baking powder and salt into bowl. Cut in butter until crumbly. Add egg; mix with fork. Press half of crumb mixture into greased 13x9x2-inch baking pan. Spoon cherry filling over first layer. Top with remaining crumbs.

Bake in 350° oven 30 minutes or until golden brown. Cool in pan on rack. Serve warm topped with whipped cream or ice cream if you wish. Makes 12 servings.

INDEX

315